Disaster Preparedness for Healthcare Facilities:
Experiences, Statistics and Solutions

Thompson Publishing Group
1725 K Street, NW
Washington, DC 20006

202-872-4000 (Editorial Offices)
1-800-677-3789 (Customer Service)

www.thompson.com

ñ THOMPSON

Disaster Preparedness for Healthcare Facilities:

Experiences, Statistics and Solutions

Disaster Preparedness for Healthcare Facilities: Experiences, Statistics and Solutions is published by Thompson Publishing Group, Inc., 1725 K St. NW, 7th Floor, Washington, DC 20006.

ISBN 1-933807-00-8
978-1-933807-00-3
Printed in the United States

This publication is designed to be accurate and authoritative, but the publisher is not rendering legal, accounting or other professional servicees. If legal or other expert advice is desired, retain the services of an appropriate professional.

Copyright © 2006 by American Health Consultants, Inc. All rights reserved.
Photocopying without the publisher's consent is strictly prohibited. Consent needs to be granted to reproduce individual items for personal or internal use by the
Copyright Clearance Center, 222 Rosewood Drive, Danvers, MA 01923.

To order additional copies of this book, please contact us:

Call: 1-800-677-3789
Online: www.thompson.com
Fax: 1-800-999-5661
Email: service@thompson.com
Mail: Thompson Publishing Group
Subscription Service Center
PO Box 26185
Tampa, FL 33623-6185

ft THOMPSON

How to Use This Book

In our world, disasters are a reality. They will occur. The real question is: Will you be ready when one hits your community?

Disaster Preparedness for Healthcare Facilities: Experiences, Statistics and Solutions is an essential sourcebook that addresses how to plan for a disaster, what to do when disaster strikes and how to deal with the aftermath. It includes case studies, examples, suggestions, and statistics on disaster planning – written just for healthcare facilities.

The expert guidance provided in this important resource is taken from the real-life experiences of professionals who have shared what worked – and didn't work – when disaster struck. Because disaster planning, at best, means dealing with probabilities and not likelihoods, it is an ever-evolving process. This book will be a valuable tool in preparing your facility for a possible disaster.

What's Inside?

With tighter regulations looming, emergency drills and disaster plans are critical to health care administration. In this book you will discover:

- tips on creating a crisis management plan;
- specific ways to prepare your facility for a natural disaster; and
- how to run and evaluate test drills.

We'll identify **integral external resources,** and give you suggestions on **creating partnerships** to bolster your plan. We'll examine **emergency decisions,** including whether or not to evacuate, coping with staffing issues, and tracking patients. **We'll provide advice on infection control** and **inspecting your facility after a disaster.** And much more.

You'll find examples, checklists, and templates on such important topics as:

- developing call trees;
- creating contingency plans;
- backing up electrical and communication services; and
- creating a disaster plan from scratch.

Our Guarantee

Please take a minute to review ***Disaster Preparedness for Healthcare Facilities: Experiences, Statistics and Solutions.*** You have our 30-day risk-free guarantee. We are confident that this sourcebook will become a trusted resource for your disaster planning and recovery program. If you don't agree, just return the book to us with the enclosed invoice.

If we can be of any assistance, please do not hesitate to contact our customer service department at 1-800-677-3789. Thank you for subscribing to Thompson's healthcare publications.

Table of Contents

Chapter 1: Before the Storm

In Disaster Planning, Imagination is Key 3

May it be Writ in Stone: Create Risk Management Proviso 5

Is Your Facility Prepared for a Disaster to Hit? 9

Take These Steps to Prepare Your Facility 13
- *Prechecklist for Facilities* 15
- *New Tool Evaluates Disaster Plans* 18

Disaster Preparedness: Lessons Learned From the
Response to Hurricane Katrina 19

The Joint Commission is Watching: Is Your Disaster
Response Plan in Order? 25

A New Compliance Reality When Disaster Strikes 29

To Evacuate or not to Evacuate? 31

Local Heroes: JCAHO Says Rural Areas Must be Ready to
Stand Alone 33

Lucky 13: Key Steps to Small-town Readiness 37

Chapter 2: In the ED

Evacuate or 'Hunker Down'? ED Experts Ponder Options
As Katrina Wreaks Havoc 45

Staffing up Helps EDs Handle Katrina Surge 49

System Addresses Ability to Transition in Emergencies 53
- *Patient Readiness Ratings* 54

System Came out of 9/11 Response 57

Lessons Learned From Hurricane Katrina: EDs Share
Their Best Disaster Strategies 61

Will You Meet the Needs of ED Nurses During Disasters? 65

Katrina-born Tracking Forms Aid Rita Response 69

Table of Contents

    Triage During a Mass Disaster: The Usual Rules Don't Apply 73

    Make Decontamination Part of All-hazards Plan 79

    When Disaster Strikes: Treating Patients When Your
        Department Shuts Down 81

    Space, Staff Key Concerns in ED Surge Capacity Plans 85

    Hospitals' Preparation for Surge of Patients Helps With
        New Joint Commission Standards 87

Chapter 3: Coping with Disaster

    Infection Control 101 for Temporary Shelters 93

    Shelter From the Storm: ICPs – A Voice of Reason in
        A Mind-numbing Disaster 99

    Failure to Provide Backup Power Results in Death
        And a $450,000 Massachusetts Settlement 105

    Larger Role in Disaster Planning Seen for Quality Managers 111

    Health Care Heroes Weather Gulf Storm with Guts and
        Emergency Planning 115

    Chief Nursing Officer Recounts Katrina Efforts 119

    Case Managers Face Challenges of Hurricane Katrina 123

    Case Study: Pensacola Hospital and Patients Survive
        Battering by Hurricane Ivan 127

    Florida Managers Deal with the Effects of
        Back-to-back Hurricanes 131

Chapter 4: Plans and Procedures

    Disaster Preparedness Plan Outline 139

    FEMA: 2005 Federal Disaster Declarations 161

    Checklist for Infection Control 165

    JCAHO Guidance on Emergency Planning 173

    Hospital Preparedness Statistics 177

    Department and Unit Disaster Sub-plan Templates 179

Before the Storm

Chapter Contents

In Disaster Planning, Imagination is Key 3

May it be Writ in Stone: Create Risk Management Proviso 5

Is Your Facility Prepared for a Disaster to Hit? 9

Take These Steps to Prepare Your Facility 13
    • *Prechecklist for Facilities* 15
    • *New Tool Evaluates Disaster Plans* 18

Disaster Preparedness: Lessons Learned From the
Response to Hurricane Katrina 19

The Joint Commission is Watching: Is Your Disaster
Response Plan in Order? 25

A New Compliance Reality When Disaster Strikes 29

To Evacuate or not to Evacuate? 31

Local Heroes: JCAHO Says Rural Areas Must be Ready to
Stand Alone 33

Lucky 13: Key Steps to Small-town Readiness 37

In Disaster Planning, Imagination is Key

As Joe Cappiello, BSN, MA, vice president of accreditation field operations for the Joint Commission, put it, the Hurricane Katrina disaster in New Orleans was really a "perfect storm" of four separate disasters. It was a confluence of events that few had foreseen, and that's all the more reason, say the experts, to let your imagination run wild when planning for disasters.

"The biggest thing is that people need to sit and talk and have a kind of twisted imagination," says Mary Frost, RN, trauma coordinator at Texas Children's Hospital in Houston. That's exactly what the city's health care community did in the wake of Hurricane Allison in 2001, creating Houston's Regional Unified Medical Command Center. The result? After Katrina hit New Orleans, Houston was deluged with about 25,000 additional hospital patients, yet almost all of the city's hospitals were kept off diversion.

"Things that seemed were the questions to ask turned out not to be; this is bigger than anything anyone else has ever seen," says William (Kip) Schumacher, MD, CEO and founder of The Schumacher Group, a Lafayette, LA-based practice management firm that provides emergency medicine, staffing, and practice management services to 104 facilities, including 30 in Louisiana, and which was heavily involved in the Katrina response process.

"It was so catastrophic, so big, that every time I thought we had a grasp on the situation I realized everything we had done was so far under what could have been done," he says.

The rules, he adds, changed totally. "They were talking about evacuating hospitals with pickup trucks, because air evacuation had difficult access," he recalls. "We had hospitals evacuated by boats that our docs were pushing and paddling."

In preparing for the unexpected, says Randy Pilgrim, MD, president and chief medical officer of The Schumacher Group, "do a number of scenarios that you can play out prior to an event, so you can understand how key decisions might be made. Know who to contact, how to get hold of them if normal communications do not work. Think of who needs to have a satellite phone now, while the storm is still coming."

Those scenarios could include evacuation of patients ahead of the storm, he says. "It may be advisable, but you have to acknowledge that there is tremendous risk in making that decision," he warns.

"It's very difficult to understand what magnitude of deficit will hit you once the storm hits," Pilgrim continues. "What is key is to prepare yourself ahead of time by orderly examination of what may happen when it hits."

For more information, contact:

- Mary Frost, RN, Trauma Coordinator, Texas Children's Hospital, 6621 Fannin St., Houston, TX 77030. Phone: (832) 824-1000.

- William (Kip) Schumacher, MD, CEO, The Schumacher Group, 200 Corporate Blvd., Suite 201, Lafayette, LA 70508. Phone: (800) 893-9698.

May it be Writ in Stone: Create Risk Management Proviso

Sooner or later, some type of crisis will hit you and your organization. It's an inevitable part of your job, so risk managers should plan for that day by preparing contingency plans and putting together a "bible" of crucial information ahead of time, suggest two risk managers who have weathered storms.

The advice comes from June Leigh, CPHRM, RN, BSN, MS, FASHRM, ARM, risk control director with CNA HealthPro in Chicago, and Nancy Lagorio, RN, MS, CCLA, risk control consultant with the company. They presented their strategies for crisis management at a meeting of the American Society of Healthcare Risk Management (ASHRM) in Orlando, FL.

A risk manager's crisis can take many forms, Leigh says, from a tornado hitting your hospital to a medical error that causes the death of a patient. "In health care, a crisis is something that suddenly or unexpectedly has actual or potential adverse effects on the organization or its patients, staff, or community," she says. "That can cover a lot of scenarios."

Leigh notes that not all crises lead to a disaster in which the organization experiences total failure. But some crises that start out relatively small can build to that point if handled poorly, she warns.

"Some organizations may manage to avoid a crisis turning into a disaster through plain old dumb luck, but more reliably, it's better to prepare and plan," Leigh says. "Like the old saying goes, 'It wasn't raining when Noah built the ark.'"

All industries have to contend with crises, but she notes that health care providers have an added burden because their crises tend to hit the front page of the newspaper, with the biggest headlines, and stay on the front page longer. They also receive both regional and national attention, a result of the public's overall level of distrust regarding health care.

"The longer the bad news stays on the TV news or on the front page, the more damage it is likely to do," Leigh says, "and the more difficult it is to overcome."

Always tell the truth

Risk managers should always keep in mind how the media will portray any action, or inaction, by the health care organization, she says. Leigh and Lagorio offer these key strategies for responding to any crisis:

- Tell the truth, tell it well, and tell it often. This is the No. 1 rule for any crisis. Refer to it when in doubt about what to say to anyone.

- Do the right thing.

- Don't delay. A crisis always requires prompt action. Doing nothing is always the worst response.

- Don't expect a crisis to go according to plan. Actual crises rarely are identical to what you prepared for. The best you can hope for is that you prepared for the general type of crisis you're facing and that your plans are flexible enough to allow you to adapt to the realities unfolding.

Include reps from all major departments

Lagorio says your crisis management plans should start with an identification of potential problems that you could face. These will differ from one organization to the next, depending partly on your geographical location, the size and type of your facility, and the services you offer.

The types of crises range from natural disasters, such as tornadoes, to external emergencies, such as a chemical exposure in the community. There also can be internal crises, such as large-scale infections. And don't forget the internal, nonmedical crises such as an employee strike.

When brainstorming about potential crises and the response plans, be sure to include a representative from every part of the organization, says Lagorio. For each potential crisis, she advises considering each of these points:

- geographic scope and duration;
- impact on operations;
- employee involvement;
- regulatory, accreditation, and law enforcement involvement;
- public concern;
- likely media coverage.

For each scenario you anticipate, carefully establish a formal crisis management and communications team with clearly defined roles and responsibilities. Be sure to consider communications facilities and the heavy demands on space, telephones, web sites, and other resources.

Develop a bible to use in a crisis

Part of your planning should include the development of a bible that can guide you through the tough times, Leigh says. Distribute this handbook of crucial information to leaders throughout the organization so that it is ready to use in a crisis. Leigh and Lagorio recommend including this information in the bible:

- Contact information for core team members, backups, and chain of command.

- Contact information for those others who need to be informed, such as sales representatives, switchboard operators, site security, and contact people at other company sites.

- Information for contacting key people outside the organization, such as experts to whom you can turn for information and external spokespersons.

- A list of local and national media contacts.

- Common questions and answers that may apply in this crisis. For a crisis involving a particular procedure, for instance, the questions might address when the procedure was approved, how many people have the disease, how many procedures are performed nationwide and at your facility each year.

Update the questions and answers frequently, but save the old ones in a separate section in case a reporter asks about information you presented previously. Reporters frequently review archived media stories and may inquire about old statistics or answers, so you need to know where that information came from.

- Any past press releases relating to the issue. Again, you need to know what you have told the press in the past, even if that information no longer is current.

- Procedures that address document management, including e-mail.

- A communication plan that addresses all major constituencies such as patients and families, internal staff, medical staff, board members, and public officials. Be sure to include your policy on who is authorized to communicate with the media or other parties.

- Procedures for media relations, including access to patients, photography, press conferences, message logs, and media inquiry forms.

- Rules for security and confidentiality, including the release of information.

- Policies on training personnel and conducting drills.

Use media to communicate your message

Rely on the bible you prepared before the crisis, but be sure to update it with relevant information during the crisis situation. Add information such as statements issued, supportive statements from third parties, media coverage, and backup information such as published studies and sources for the statistics you will quote.

A major part of your crisis management plan should involve how you communicate internally and to the public. She advises following these key steps for crisis communication:

1. Gather the facts
2. Determine the size of the crisis
3. Assemble those involved
4. Delegate assignments
5. Relate the facts promptly
6. Communicate from a high level
7. Accept responsibility but not blame
8. Express compassion
9. Use your positive reputation to your advantage
10. Follow up with more communications after the crisis to rebuild the image of your organization and restore public trust

Is Your Facility Prepared for a Disaster To Hit?

Is your center prepared for a disaster that could cause you to close your doors, contact patients and staff, and later reopen safely? Information from centers that have weathered hurricanes in Florida can apply to any disaster.

Perform disaster drills

At Kissimmee (FL) Surgery Center, disaster drills cover weather scenarios, terrorism, and building damage from car accidents, says Lou Warmijak, administrator.

Some drills include full evacuations, Warmijak says. "You can never be too prepared," he adds.

Some drills are held using an actual patient and his or her family, Warmijak says. Patients are selected from those least likely to be upset by a drill, such as repeat endoscopy or pain management patients and families of firefighters and police officers. The drill is held after the patient is ready for discharge. After the drill, patients and families are asked what made them anxious and how they thought the staff handled the situation. Ancillary staff members fill in as pseudo patients in the drills.

Obtain business interruption insurance

Kissimmee Surgery Center lost six days of business in the fall of 2004 due to hurricanes, Warmijak says. About 50% of those cases have been rescheduled, he says.

The corporation that owns his center does have business interruption insurance, and his center was responsible for evaluating how much of its losses, including payroll, additional supply costs, and lost surgery, would be covered. "But it covers pretty much everything you lose during down time," Warmijak says.

Have systems in place to communicate with patients and staff

When you know a potential disaster is coming, such as a hurricane, verify your phone numbers for your key contacts, advises William Phillips, PhD, president of Riteway Services, a Winter Park, FL-based business that handles facilities management for ambulatory surgery centers.

"Make sure the numbers you have are actually good numbers," Phillips says.

Administrators and key contacts need to make sure they have a traditional telephone at their addresses that does not work from electrical power, he says. After the hurricanes, cell phone coverage was poor, and cordless phones weren't working because the electricity was off, he says.

Keep in mind that patients who live outside of your immediate area might not be affected by a disaster such as hurricane and may not realize afterward that you are closed, Warmijak points out. Also, roads may be unsafe due to downed power lines or debris. "That is another responsibility: to communicate with these individuals," he says.

At Kissimmee Surgery Center, when a potential disaster such as a hurricane is predicted, patients are contacted to determine if they want to continue with the procedure if the center is up and running, Warmijak says.

"A lot of them want to go through with the surgery," he says. However, keep in mind that some patients may not have power after a disaster, which might make their homes less than ideal for recovery, sources say.

Staff members verify the patients' phone numbers, including cell phone numbers, and give them an anticipated time to hear from the center staff. "We tell them how to call the building, and we tell them if the answering machine doesn't come on, you know the building doesn't have phones and electricity," Warmijak says.

Also, for patients who live near the center, they are told that information about opening the facility will be posted on the front of the building or somewhere on the building.

The center has assigned its staff to teams that handle different levels of communication. For example, the business office team copies and carries home three to five days of schedules, including patients' and physicians' contact numbers. The materials manager communicates with vendors to let them know if the center is closed, when they expect to open, and to determine if there are any expected delays in shipments. Due to storm damage, some shipping services may not be available.

Evaluate damage after disaster

If you turned off the power before a potential disaster, have the building cleared of any structural or electrical problems before you turn it back on, Warmijak says.

Have an architect or a general contractor walk through the facility within hours of the disaster, Phillips advises. Also, have an electrician check the power status, he suggests.

"Make sure the voltage is correct and all phases are correct," Phillips says. ⋔

For more information, contact:

- Kay Beauregard, RN, MSA, Director of Hospital Accreditation and Nursing Quality, William Beaumont Hospital, 3601 W 13 Mile Rd., Royal Oak, MI 48073. Phone: (248) 898-0941. E-mail: kbeauregard@beaumont.edu.

- William Cassidy, MD, Associate Professor of Medicine, LSU Health Science Center, Baton Rouge, LA. E-mail: wcassi@lsuhsc.edu.

- Joe Cappiello, BSN, MA, Vice President, Accreditation Field Operations, Joint Commission on Accreditation of Healthcare Organizations, One Renaissance Blvd., Oakbrook Terrace, IL 60181. Phone: (630) 792-5000.

Take These Steps to Prepare Your Facility

There are several steps you can take before a storm to ensure your building and its contents are protected, says William Phillips, PhD, president of Riteway Services, a Winter Park, FL-based business that handles facilities management for ambulatory surgery centers.

Riteway Services has a prechecklist for facilities. **(See page 15.)** If a hurricane approaches that is expected to be a Category 2 or above, facilities shut off their generators to secure power for later, Phillips says.

In preparation for Hurricane Francis, Kissimmee (FL) Surgery Center prepared for a Category 3 hurricane, which meant turning off all power. Once the power is turned off, heat and humidity build up in the facility, and all sterile packages must be resterilized, says Lou Warmijak, administrator.

Also, medications that need to be refrigerated will need to be stored when power is turned off, Phillips points out. Store them in dry ice or regular ice in a 90-hour cooler, he suggests. "Once you pack them, suck the air off them with a portable vacuum," Phillips advises.

Planning for Hurricane Jeanne

After the facility finished with the last patient of the day, all equipment was to be covered, and everything essential was to be moved off the floor, Warmijak said. Trash bags were going to be used to cover all electronic equipment and operating room equipment, and the equipment was going to be moved into rooms with no windows.

All computerized data were to be backed up and moved off-site into waterproof areas, adds Warmijak. In addition, items could be stored in waterproof safes and also were moved to secure locations owned by the hospital company that owns the center, he notes.

The managers were devising a plan that included a time to check out the building, post-disaster, Warmijak said.

"That's when the response is put out to staff that the building is open and we're ready to work, or we're closed and they should wait to hear from us," he says.

After Hurricane Charley, the center had no electricity or phones, so the leaders posted a notice on the building about the situation and the anticipated return of electricity, Warmijak says.

Keep in mind that if your telephone system goes without power for 72 hours, it may lose its programming, Phillips points out. Add remote access terminals and download the telephone program before a disaster, so you can access the telephone programming from your facility's computer later, if needed, he suggests.

This process can be handled by your telecommunications provider and takes about 15 minutes, Phillips says. "The cost is minor compared to someone sitting there and reprogramming your system for two days," he adds.

Also, install phase monitors on all air-conditioning units and vacuum pumps, Phillips advises. The monitor will prevent your power from restoring if the voltage or phase is not correct, he says. Air-conditioning or electrical contractors can provide those monitors for about $75 per installation, Phillips says. "That's not too bad, considering that otherwise you may lose a motor that, in a disaster situation, may take you a week to get."

There are automatic and manual phase monitors, Phillips says. "We always use the automatic," he says. "If we have a lockout situation [with the power], we don't know when that will occur, and we're not sure when it will be restored." Those systems also work well for thunderstorms, he points out.

Also have a prearranged contract for debris cleanup before a hurricane actually hits, Phillips advises. "After the storm hits, you can get to work, and they're cleaned up right after the storm," he says. 🏠

Prechecklist for Facilities

Severe Weather Preparation

rev 9.03

FACILITY _____ DATE _____

Admin Verify	Assigned Task	Action Check	Description	Staff initial

FACILITY PREPARATION

			FACILITY STATUS. Event is after hours or the facility operation has already been determined to be closed.	
			TELEPHONE MESSAGE. Program message at the facility, advising callers of facility status.	
			INSPECT EXTERIOR. Move all loose material such as chairs and construction material from the site or to a secure location.	
			CONSTRUCTION ONGOING. Advise all contractors to secure the construction site and materials and construction entrances or storage areas.	
			LAB SAMPLE BOXES. Take in all lab specimen boxes from outside to the interior of the facility.	
			PATIENTS AND MEDICAL STAFF. Determine closing items and notify patients and medical staff as necessary. Cover with plastic as added precaution from water damage or intrusion.	
			SUPPLIES/TRASH. Put up all supplies and remove all trash from the facility into proper containers. Close gates and covers on all receptacle areas as equipped.	
			ROOFTOP EQUIPMENT. Ensure that the equipment is properly secured and all panels are securely fastened.	
			INSPECT ROOF. Clear off all material on the roof that could be made airborne. Inspect all mechanical equipment and ensure all covers are in place and screwed tightly.	

HIGH WIND PROTECTION

			EXTERIOR WINDOWS AND DOORS. Commercial grade. Inspect all windows and doors for cracking or damage prior to storm. Secure as necessary.	
			STOREFRONTS and AUTOMATIC DOORS. Lock and secure doors and operators. Tape all openings and cracks to avoid wind-driven water intrusion.	
			INTERIOR PREPARATION. Move all furnishings from window areas to interior walls.	

Chapter 1: Before the Storm

FACILITY _____ DATE _____					
Admin Verify	**Assigned Task**	**Action Check**	**Description**		**Staff initial**
			INTERIOR PREPARATION. Move all medical equipment away form building exterior window walls to interior protected walls.		
			PATIENT RECORDS. Secure all patient records and charts in a secure location within the records department as needed.		
			INTERIOR PREPARATION. Place collection containers beneath all equipment penetrations, roof drains, and known leak areas.		

ELECTRICAL PROTECTION

			CONNECTION MODERATE TO LOW PREVALENCE OF UTILITY DAMAGE HURRICANE 2 OR BELOW		
			Unplug all non-essential medical equipment and bring to interior walls. Includes anesthesia machines, patient monitors, X-ray, and all connected equipment.		
			SEVERE HIGH WINDS. Cover all computers and electrical equipment / medical equipment with plastic as added protection from overhead water intrusion in the event of a building electrical failure.		
			TELEPHONE EQUIPMENT. If not protected by a surge suppressor or UPS disconnect use emergency mailbox to leave message provided by utility carrier.		
			COMPUTERS. Shut down all computers in all areas. Secure the server routers and microwave equipment.		
			HVAC EQUIPMENT. Secure and shut down all refrigeration sections of unprotected rooftop equipment. Unprotected equipment is any equipment without separate phase monitors installed for three phase electrical-operated equipment.		
			LIGHTING. Secure all lighting except life safety lighting circuits.		
			EQUIPMENT. Secure all equipment prior to leaving the facility. Shut down air compressors, vacuum system equipment, sterilizers, and boilers.		
			MEDICAL GAS. Secure all medical gas system services. Disconnect anesthesia machines and turn all equipment off.		
			CONDITION HIGH WIND AND SEVERE DAMAGE LIKELY HURRICANE 3 AND ABOVE		

FACILITY _____ DATE _____					
Admin Verify	**Assigned Task**	**Action Check**	**Description**		**Staff initial**
			Comply with all actions above and turn the generator control to off. (Emergency power will not come on when left in this condition.)	
			Secure all mechanical equipment and rooftop ventilation equipment.	
			For duration of the storm log off fire alarm and security systems.	
			Outage planned for 24 hours or less before restoration. Remove all frozen and refrigerated medications and cold packs in coolers within the facility. Place in isolated interior location and clearly label for restocking.	

MISCELLANEOUS ALL CONDITIONS

	RWS*		Notify security company to only report alarms with perimeter and motion sensor combined signals.
	RWS*		Refuel and top off generators.
	RWS*		Inspect areas for compliance exterior and interior.
	RWS*		Ensure all trash is removed from facility.
*Riteway Services Inc.			

Tips

Remember whenever you call someone to leave a message or obtain a status advisory leave the numbers you can be called back at.

As a KEY CONTACT make certain you have a telephone at home that will work without being plugged into an electrical circuit.

CHARGE ALL CELLULAR PHONES AND EXTRA BATTERIES.

If medications and tissues are cold packed have at least three to four knowledgable people to respond on call back to replace these items in the refrigerators and freezers. In the event of a severe storm some people may not be able to communicate or get out of their homes for several days.

NEW TOOL EVALUATES DISASTER PLANS

The Agency for Healthcare Research and Quality (AHRQ) has produced an evidence-based tool to help hospitals evaluate their disaster training drills. Called "Evaluation of Hospital Disaster Drills: A Module-Based Approach," it is designed to help hospitals identify strengths and weaknesses in their responses during a disaster drill.

The tool is based on several key principles, including the need to plan drill objectives, train observers, document drill activities, and debrief all participants. Its evaluation modules are designed to capture all phases of drill activities, such as pre-drill planning and recording activities in each area of the hospital including incident command, decontamination, triage, and treatment.

The tool is available from the agency as a notebook with accompanying CD-ROM. The CD version of the modules includes a spreadsheet designed to help compile responses from the modules and compare data on topics such as how the hospital performs on repeated exercises, how different parts of the hospital perform on the same factors, or how different hospitals perform when participating in the same drill.

Copies of the tool are available at no charge on the AHRQ web site: http://www.ahrq.gov/research/hospdrills/. If you have any questions about AHRQ's bioterrorism and health system preparedness program, contact: Sally Phillips, MD, Director, Bioterrorism Preparedness Research Program, Center for Primary Care, Prevention, and Clinical Partnerships. Phone: (301) 427-1571. E-mail: SPhillip@ahrq.gov.

Disaster Preparedness: Lessons Learned From the Response to Hurricane Katrina

Your recent disaster drills may have prepared you for scenarios such as local school bus accidents, an explosion at a nearby plant, or chemical spills at a factory.

But what about a disaster of epic proportions that leaves your hospital structurally damaged, with no power for days? Or a bioterrorism attack that paralyzes every community resource in the surrounding area?

The lesson to learn from Hurricane Katrina, which struck in the late summer of 2005: Think big. When doing a hazards vulnerability analysis to determine which disasters are most likely to strike, your organization must consider major catastrophes and large-scale events, says Robert Wise, MD, vice president of the division of standards and survey methods for the Joint Commission on Accreditation of Healthcare Organizations (JCAHO).

"I think organizations have been timid in being clear about the hazards that might occur to them," he says. "Because if, in fact, it's decided that they have to prepare for a significant hazard, then obviously there are potentially significant expenses associated with that."

Typically, the hazards most frequently prepared for are those that have already occurred, says Wise. "That makes sense, but at the same time, the catastrophic ones also have to be at least considered," he says.

Every disaster presents a learning opportunity, says Wise, who visited the Gulf region to meet with affected health care organizations. "We typically go to the area about six or eight weeks after the disaster, when things have calmed down, and will do this with New Orleans and Mississippi. But it is way too premature to seek lessons learned at this point," he says.

One of the biggest lessons is already readily apparent, however; the more planning an organization does, the better. "All the resources invested in planning will be paid for many times over when the actual disaster occurs," says Jonathan Weisul, MD, vice president of medical affairs for Alexandria, LA-based Christus St. Frances Cabrini Hospital. Weisul is responsible for JCAHO compliance for Christus Health's Central Louisiana region. "This was a response of unprecedented dimensions, and the follow-up and after action will be created as we go."

Although the hospital wasn't directly affected by Katrina, over several days 700 patients were triaged and hundreds were hospitalized. At one point, the hospital's Mass Casualty Incident plan was activated after buses with 100 patients arrived with less than 30 minutes notice. "In that experience, the disaster plan worked extremely well. We were able to triage and place the patients within four hours. That included one fatality that died on the way, but other adverse outcomes could have occurred if the plan hadn't worked as well."

"I don't think quality has been addressed until recently in emergency management," says Victor H. Kennedy, MPH, CIH, director and health care system safety officer at UCLA Medical Center in Los Angeles. "The planning and drill efforts didn't go beyond the initial response."

That is changing now, he says, pointing to the Joint Commission's emergency management standards, which state that they reflect "the application of continuous quality improvement methods to the performance of emergency management preparation."

New emphasis on quality

"In the new JCAHO standards, there is a good bit of talk about quality. JCAHO has given justification" to a new emphasis on quality, he says.

This means that organizations will need to "push the envelope" when evaluating drills to ensure that quality has been assessed and maintained, says Kennedy. Drills typically end after three or four hours, but the window of time for evaluation should be expanded to measure the quality of care given to patients, he argues.

"We typically don't talk about the degree of quality care we provide to victims. It is easier to talk about mobilization and logistics – whether you got the lights on – than quality."

Ask these two questions after drills, he recommends: How effective was your response? Did you meet your overall objective of continuing to care for patients, and responding to the health care needs of the community?

"We have been discussing this here," Kennedy says. "First, you need to include individuals who are used to measuring those kinds of outcomes, including quality managers."

One possibility is that the first part of a drill could assess the initial response, while a second part could assess follow-up and quality issues, he suggests. "The earthquake happens, you respond, then you take a break and pretend it's two days later," Kennedy says. "We would follow up with the patients as we do our normal patients. We have a mechanism for that during normal operations, but do we have a mechanism to do that during a disaster?"

He points to the Joint Commission's four required elements for an emergency management plan: preparedness, mitigation, response, and recovery. "Following up is part of recovery and is only now getting attention in health care," he says.

"In the past, disaster planning was done mainly to maintain accreditation and meet JCAHO standards," says Weisul.

That is no longer the case, as organizations have made disaster planning a priority and allocated significant resources for drills and planning exercises, says Kennedy. "If something happens, it's not going to be the safety guy in front of the news media, it's going to be the CEO," he adds.

Look outside your organization

However, many organizations still don't participate in disaster planning on a communitywide level, says Wise. "That is one area that continues to be difficult, so we continue to emphasize it," he says. "We are strongly urging – in fact, there is an expectation – that hospitals reach out to the community to find out the role they should be playing.

"If the community is hit by something major and there is no electricity or water or sewage – to have a single hospital prepare for that without having its assets integrated into the overall community plan is not going to make sense," he says.

Participate in community drills, which tend to be tabletops, and invite community planners to your drills, Wise recommends. "It certainly makes sense to invite the community in. We often find, though, that they get invited to so many places they may be more reticent to get involved with individual drills. The expectation is that the hospital gets involved in the community drills."

Organizations can do this by committing their personnel, time, and resources to participate with involvement of quality leaders, says Weisul. "Participate in the network and establish personal relationships, which are crucial in the time of a disaster," he recommends.

JCAHO surveyors will be asking, "Do you know the names of the emergency management people in the community? Are you participating in meetings? Are you aware of your role in a disaster and how communication will occur?"

Use large-scale approach

"These are the types of questions that one would want to be able to answer," says Wise. "If you can't answer those, then you haven't done adequate planning. The time to start exchanging business cards is not at the time of the disaster."

When doing your hazard vulnerability analysis, take into account that other resources in your community may be affected, as with the 9/11 terrorist attacks and Hurricane Katrina. "Over the last several years, we have seen some pretty significant disasters, including the loss of electricity in the Northeast and the hurricanes in Florida [in 2004]," Wise says. "We have now seen that organizations may in fact be on their own for long periods of time."

Disaster drills are typically geared toward a short period of time, but your organization may need to stand alone for several days, so you must address emergency power, water, sewage, and personnel issues, says Wise. "To be able to sustain an organization for several days without any outside help and build that kind of infrastructure is actually quite expensive," he says. "That's why you need to sit down with the community to figure out which medical resources are going to be able to stay up and running, and if organizations need to evacuate, where they would go."

After each drill, an after-action analysis should be done to identify weaknesses and vulnerable areas, says Weisul. "You need to keep asking, 'What if? What if the backup power went down? What if patients arrive with no notice and helicopters were landing without any contact?'" he asks.

At UCLA, every drill generates a written critique and detailed action plan given to the disaster committee, which is chaired by a physician. "It is part of the medical staff executive committee, which gives it a lot more power and makes sure the action plan stays on the agenda until the issues are resolved," says Kennedy. "Then we test them again to see if we actually did fix them."

Identifying backup plans for communication is essential, says Weisul. "Communication during a disaster is crucial," he adds. "One of the difficulties of a true disaster is that information is inadequate or changes by the moment."

During Katrina, cell phones weren't working since the system was quickly overwhelmed. As a result, St. Frances Cabrini developed plans to use two-way radios as its primary form of communication during disasters. "The ability to communicate with the affected hospitals in New Orleans was reduced to ham radios," adds Weisul. "Hospitals should consider having access to ham radio operators and equipment during a disaster scenario."

Chapter 1: Before the Storm

During Katrina, an incident command center was established early on, allowing the organization to handle internal and external communications through one central source, acquire and access resources, and participate in the statewide response to the disaster.

According to Weisul, "An incident command center should be a crucial part of disaster planning and drills, because it will become the hub of all communications."

Katrina underscores the need to incorporate evacuation scenarios into your disaster drills. "It does point out to hospitals the need to truly identify and test how you are going to evacuate patients," Kennedy says. "Not just how to move them, but once you get them where they are going, how are you going to continue to provide for their care?"

During a recent drill, the organization used the scenario of a fire down the hall from the operating rooms, done after hours. "We put patient volunteers in each of our 23 ORs and pretended they had five minutes to leave," he says.

During other drills, the organization has practiced moving patients from one wing to another and relocating psychiatric patients. "We try to have a patient movement element to each of our drills," says Kennedy.

In addition, there may be two or more steps involved in moving patients during a disaster, says Kennedy. "You don't just move them from their point of origin to where care will be provided. You may be moving them outside of the immediately dangerous area, then from that staging area to their final destination," he says. "So there may be incremental steps to evacuation."

The organization's disaster plan was updated to address this scenario, by identifying specific departments that will formulate a plan for moving patients at a moment's notice if needed, including bed control, nursing, engineering, central supply, and respiratory therapy. "That group comes together and within five to 10 minutes, they will give the plan to the incident commander about how patients will be moved and where," says Kennedy.

If you know a storm is coming, as many patients as possible should be discharged, says Jeanne Eckes-Roper, RN, director of emergency preparedness for the North Broward (FL) Hospital District. If an evacuation is going to occur, the hospital should make copies of all medical records and be prepared to send all records, films, medications, and anything else needed for patient care to the receiving facility, she advises.

"Appropriate family notifications need to be done in advance of any evacuation, if possible," adds Eckes-Roper. "Patient tracking during evacuation will be a critical key for families and facilities."

Patient tracking is a concern during any disaster, even if evacuation is not required. After multiple victims were brought to the hospital after a motor vehicle crash, Kennedy realized that one patient had four identifiers: a triage number given in the field, a patient identification number assigned upon arrival to the ED, and was referred to as "the boy with the head injury" and "boy with the blue jacket."

"We got together with quality management and said, we can't have a patient with four identifiers, especially if blood or X-rays are needed," says Kennedy. "Now, when a patient comes in, they get an identifier that cross-references them wherever they go."

For more information, contact:

- Jeanne Eckes-Roper, RN, Director of Emergency Preparedness, North Broward Hospital District, 303 SE 17th St., Fort Lauderdale, FL 33316. E-mail: JECKES@nbhd.org.

- Victor H. Kennedy, MPH, CIH, Director, Healthcare System Safety Officer, UCLA Safety Office, 200 UCLA Medical Plaza, Suite 202, Los Angeles, CA 90095-6926. Phone: (310) 825-4012. E-mail: VKennedy@mednet.ucla.edu.

- Jonathan Weisul, MD, Vice President of Medical Affairs, Christus St. Frances Cabrini Hospital, 3300 Masonic Drive, Alexandria, LA 71301. Phone: (318) 561-4135. E-mail: weisul@maui.net.

The Joint Commission is Watching: Is Your Disaster Response Plan in Order?

So you've worked long and hard at putting an effective plan in place to respond to emergency incidents, and you feel you're as prepared as you can possibly be. Then, the attorney general comes on the TV and says there's an increased threat of a terrorist attack, and we all need to be better prepared. You look at the tube in frustration and say, "But I've done everything I can!" ... But have you?

"Is every single hospital in the United States perfectly prepared? I would be silly if I said yes," said Charles A. Schable, MS, director of the National Center for Infectious Diseases, Centers for Disease Control and Prevention (CDC).[1]

The Joint Commission on Accreditation of Healthcare Organizations now requires hospitals to implement their emergency management approach through a Hospital Emergency Incident Command System (HEICS), and preparedness is an area of focus for surveyors, says Steven J. Davidson, MD, MBA, FACEP, chairman of the department of emergency medicine at Maimonides Medical Center in New York City.

"Presuming that people have implemented a HEICS, they now have the opportunity to operate it with regularity," Davidson advises.

HEICS is a generic crisis management plan expressly for comprehensive medical facilities; it is modeled closely after the Fire Service Incident Command System. HEICS was created in the 1960s to help multiple agencies work together to deal with disasters such as wildfires. Davidson's own hospital completed a switch to HEICS in June 2004.

It is imperative for ED managers to revisit their major incident plans, agrees James J. Augustine, MD, FACEP, vice chair of clinical operations in the department of emergency medicine at Emory University in Atlanta and director of clinical operations at EMP, a physicians group based in Canton, OH.

Broaden your horizons

To be adequately prepared for a disaster, take these steps:

Prepare for various levels of incidents

ED managers need to look beyond a repeat of 9/11, Augustine warns. The world is different now, he says. Bioterrorism and dirty bomb plots are real, he adds.

Chapter 1: Before the Storm

"We ask ED managers to broaden their horizons and be able to apply a little more science to how we face challenging patient encounters," he says. "Our plan has to include events where something terribly unexpected happens." These can include events such as a tornado striking the area or a major train derailment/hazardous material release.

But preparation should not be limited to only the most serious incidents, adds Davidson. "Hospital systems can, and should be, prepared at levels appropriate to occurrences, and those may happen at a Level 1 or where there's an incident with potential for producing casualties that don't happen, like a severe thunderstorm watch, where you also could lose power," he explains.

A fire alarm in the hospital also can spur a Level 1 activation of HEICS, he says. "This begins preparing the organization for thinking in this way and becoming fluent in communicating through the system should bigger things happen," he explains.

Each level of HEICS hones preparedness that much more, Davidson says. For example, Level 2 presupposes a minor impact on hospital operations. "It may be nothing more than holding more patients than anticipated in an overcrowded ER," he notes.

But such all-level preparedness is critical, says Davidson. "You are appropriately rehearsing, and as an ED leader, that is your case to make to your management: 'Let's activate HEICS in Level 1 every time we know we're having a bad thunderstorm.' In other words, 'Let's practice.'"

Augustine agrees with the importance of practice. "Have every department in your hospital conduct at least a small drill," he says.

Reassure staff about safety and communication

In times of increased danger, it also is important to reassure staff, says Augustine. "It's appropriate to let staff know that everything will be done to protect their safety," he advises.

Provide this reassurance on an everyday basis, with scourges such as tuberculosis or methicillin-resistant Staphylococcus aureus. "Make sure you have developed a good security plan and good lockdown procedures and have a communication plan that assures staff you will be able to get a hold of them," Augustine says.

"Every hospital and ED leader should understand what type of incident would automatically require him/her to report to the hospital," he explains.

"That response should be trained down to 'X' level of personnel in the leadership path."

The largest incidents should result in an automatic response of every clinical member of the ED, says Augustine. "Then the department staff would organize themselves and specifically send some people to sleep somewhere in the hospital, to make sure a few 'fresh bodies' are available to work the shift in 12 hours," he notes.

Other incidents may require the hospital to notify staff through the electronic media, Augustine says. Some hospitals and communities have pager systems that are more durable and would be functional even if phones are incapacitated, he adds. "Other incidents which involve the hospital, but not the community at large, would require the hospital to use local police or EMS to notify important ED leaders and have them report for duty," he says.

When preparing your staff, Augustine says, the message should be simple: "Even if the phones fail, you will know when it's time to come in; you will be safe, and we will provide a way for you to provide excellent care."

Obtain buy-in from administration for hospitalwide preparation

Finally, advises Davidson, don't think of your department as separate and apart from the rest of the hospital. "If your hospital leadership is not willing to do what should be done in working through these [different levels of disaster drills], the ED will not be getting the practice it requires," he says.

ED management leadership should be teaching that lesson to the hospital leadership, Davidson maintains.

"The ED can't be rehearsing in isolation," he adds. ñ

For more on major incident response plans, contact:

- James J. Augustine, MD, FACEP, Director, Clinical Operations, EMP, 4535 Dressler Road, Canton, OH 44718. Phone: (330) 493-4443. E-mail: Jaugust@ emory.edu.

- Steven J. Davidson, MD, MBA, Chair, Emergency Medicine, Maimonides Medical Center, 4802 10th Ave., Brooklyn, NY 11219. Phone: (718) 283-6030/ 6042 (voice/fax). E-mail: Davidson@pobox.com.

Reference

1. *CNN Saturday Morning News,* June 5, 2004.

A New Compliance Reality When Disaster Strikes

Quality managers involved in disaster planning and response should not be overly concerned with following the letter of compliance law if a disaster occurs, says Joe Cappiello, BSN, MA, vice president of accreditation field operations, for the Joint Commission on Accreditation of Healthcare Organizations (JCAHO).

"The emphasis is not so much on the written plan, because it becomes moot in minutes," he notes. "It's the thoughtful process and communication that goes into the preparation, and the things you learn from drilling that allow you to adapt to situations that present themselves."

A disaster is not the time to wonder if you are in 100% compliance, he continues. "But we still expect that as a facility responds to a particular event there is a thought of how to provide the safest, best care in the most reasonable environment possible. In the first minutes right after the disaster, when you are looking at survival and preservation of the facility, that's hard, but when the dust sort of settles and you realize you have a large number of casualties, and you may have to expand to the surge facility outside of the medical center, you have to start thinking of how you can give the best care possible under such circumstances."

Key roles for quality

One of the key roles the quality manager can play, he says, "is to help keep the ethical, moral, realistic compass pointed in the right direction. Act as a supporter for the staff as they start to think things through."

Government agencies clearly recognize that full compliance is not possible during disasters. Shortly after Katrina hit the Gulf Coast, for example, the Centers for Medicare & Medicaid Services (CMS) acted to assure that Medicare, Medicaid, and the State Children's Health Insurance Program (SCHIP) would flex to accommodate the emergency health care needs of beneficiaries and medical providers in the Hurricane Katrina-devastated states.

Many of the programs' normal operating procedures were relaxed. For example, CMS announced that:

- Normal licensing requirements for doctors, nurses, and other health care professionals who cross state lines to provide emergency care in stricken areas would be waived as long as the provider was licensed in their home state.

- Health care providers that furnish medical services in good faith but cannot comply with normal program requirements because of Hurricane Katrina would be paid for services provided and would be exempt from sanctions for noncompliance, unless it was discovered that fraud or abuse occurred.

- Crisis services provided to Medicare and Medicaid patients who have been transferred to facilities not certified to participate in the programs would be paid.

- Programs would reimburse facilities for providing dialysis to patients with kidney failure in alternative settings.

- Normal prior authorization and out-of-network requirements also would be waived for enrollees of Medicare, Medicaid, or SCHIP managed care plans.

- Certain HIPAA privacy requirements would be waived so that health care providers could talk to family members about a patient's condition even if that patient was unable to grant that permission to the provider.

- Hospitals and other facilities could be flexible in billing for beds that have been dedicated to other uses (for example, if a psychiatric unit bed was used for an acute care patient admitted during the crisis).

- Hospital emergency departments would not be held liable under the Emergency Medical Treatment and Labor Act for transferring patients to other facilities for assessment, if the original facility was in the area where a public health emergency had been declared.

In times like these, Cappiello concludes, it's most important to keep things in perspective. "Just don't throw the standards away and say all bets are off," he advises. "You still have a moral and ethical responsibility to provide the best possible care given the circumstances."

To Evacuate or not to Evacuate?

Whether to evacuate patients prior to the arrival of a storm such as the 2005 Gulf Coast hurricanes often is not a cut-and-dried decision, says Robert Wise, MD, vice president, division of standards and survey methods for the Joint Commission on Accreditation of Healthcare Organizations (JCAHO).

"There are two kinds of decisions that need to be made," he says. "The first is at the community level, where the municipality determines whether the population should evacuate. Then, the actual hospital has to decide essentially if it is going to evacuate patients. A lot has to do with the physical facility and the hospital's ability to withstand being isolated."

In discussions with facilities in areas that get hit by hurricanes on a regular basis, says Wise, "Many have hardened their structures to handle the assault a hurricane can deliver." The most critical considerations, he says, include whether the generators can continue to operate, whether there is a water supply, and whether staff will remain available.

Of course, if your facility is about to be hit by a Category 5 storm, much depends on whether the facility itself can sustain the blow. "The vulnerability of a hospital is based on the actual structure itself and whether it can endure," Wise says. "The other part is whether it can maintain operations. The most important piece in that equation is the generators."

Water and staff

Some hospitals, he notes, have moved their generators to higher floors, to avoid flood waters. "This makes sense," he says, "But if you go back to [tropical storm] Allison in Houston [in 2001], a lot of hospitals had their generators on the third or fourth floor, but they had the switching components in the basement. You can't have any critical components on the lower floors."

Another consideration, says Wise, is how long you expect to depend on your generators for electrical power. "A typical generator is not meant to hold a hospital for several weeks at a time," he points out.

If you know your facility can withstand the storm, the other key questions involve water and staff. Having potable water and being able to maintain sanitary conditions are essential. It is also, of course, impossible to run a facility without staff. "They are devastated, too," says Wise, "Because they may have lost all their belongings. You can have a facility that is able to run, but [it can't run] if you have a staff that feels it has to go home and take care of its own needs."

How do you overcome this problem? "Some hospitals put together crews to protect staff houses," says Wise.

The bottom line is that evacuation is never an easy decision, says Randy Pilgrim, MD, president and chief medical officer of The Schumacher Group, a Lafayette, LA-based practice management firm that provides emergency medicine, staffing, and practice management services to 104 facilities, including 30 in Louisiana, and which was heavily involved the Katrina response process. He says his experiences have taught him a valuable lesson.

"I think that the biggest opportunity for change lies in having a clear idea of not necessarily when you'll make the decision but how the different ingredients of command and control will come together when the decision is imminent," says Pilgrim. "What I noticed is that there are incredible pressures on the leadership structure, given that health care is thought of in America as nearly an inalienable right and the last thing you want to take from people. That mindset leads to the fact that hospitals will stay open long past when other businesses would have closed, shut down, boarded up, and evacuated. As you do that, more chaos surrounds you. In that confusion, you must have great clarity of thought and input."

For more information, contact:

- Robert Wise, MD, Vice President, Division of Standards and Survey Methods, Joint Commission on Accreditation of Healthcare Organizations, One Renaissance Blvd., Oakbrook Terrace, IL 60181. Phone: (630) 792-5000.

- Randy Pilgrim, MD, President and Chief Medical Officer, The Schumacher Group, 200 Corporate Blvd., Suite 201, Lafayette, LA 70508. Phone: (800) 893-9698.

Local Heroes: JCAHO Says Rural Areas Must be Ready to Stand Alone

As the aftermath of Hurricane Katrina so dramatically showed, the initial community response to a natural disaster or terrorist attack has to be local.

"Like politics, every disaster is local," says Joe Cappiello, vice president for accreditation field operations at the Joint Commission on Accreditation of Healthcare Organizations (JCAHO). "The community preparedness plan cannot say, 'If we have a disaster we will hold our breath until the cavalry comes.' That is not a plan."

While large cities have all-hazard disaster plans in place in the wake of 9/11, small communities may be relatively unprepared for a catastrophic event. To address that need, JCAHO published a step-by-step guide, "Standing Together: An Emergency Planning Guide for America's Communities," to help small, rural, and suburban communities respond to major local and regional emergencies.

The planning is applicable to a variety of events, including hurricanes, floods, terrorist attacks, major infectious outbreaks, hazardous materials spills, or other catastrophic occurrences. The document emphasizes two planning strategies of particular significance to small, rural, and suburban communities. The first is to enable people to care for themselves, and the second is to build on existing relationships.

"We're trying to prepare communities to stand alone if necessary," Cappiello says. "The magic hour, the accepted [time frame] is 72 hours. If you can get past the 72-hour mark there is a pretty good chance that the state and federal government will be able to muster some resources to support you."

Many small communities in the United States struggle with emergency preparedness because they face common barriers. Those include lack of clarity about who is responsible for preparedness and response planning, what elements of the planning and response processes are critical, how to coordinate with state and federal emergency management programs, and how to obtain and sustain funding, JCAHO reports.

The JCAHO document is designed to remove such barriers by providing expert guidance on the emergency management planning process. The target audience is local leaders, including elected or appointed officials, health care practitioners and providers, and public health leaders.

"Our point of view comes from health care, but over the years, as we have looked at our emergency management standards and tried to think about how health care can be better prepared to deal with the issues of its community, it became apparent that the issue is the community," he says. "No matter what level of [accreditation] standards or requirements we put on health care, if there isn't connectivity between health care and the community it is all for naught."

To develop the document, JCAHO partnered with the Illinois Department of Public Health, the Maryland Institute of Emergency Medical Services Systems, and the National Center for Emergency Preparedness at Columbia University and convened two expert roundtable meetings in May and October 2004. The meetings addressed the issue of emergency management planning in small, rural, and suburban communities; synthesized the challenges; and framed potential solutions. That resulted in the listing of 13 key preparedness components for small communities.

Planning that prepares the community to help itself can serve to reduce the potential surge in demand for services experienced during an actual emergency, JCAHO emphasizes. The plan needs to include a well-defined risk communication plan that contains information on the guidance that will be provided to the public and how that guidance will occur (for example, distribution of flyers or other written material or public service announcements on local radio and television stations).

Some types of emergencies can be managed in homes with proper information, such as how to prevent and treat influenza in low-risk individuals during an outbreak in the community. For certain kinds of chemical exposures, the instruction to stay at home and take a shower rather than go to the hospital to be decontaminated is appropriate, JCAHO's plan states. Other types of emergencies will require mass evacuation, which is best supported by ongoing public communication, education, testing, and drills. With regard to the latter, many small communities may actually have disaster plans but typically few drills are conducted.

"It is partly a resource problem," Cappiello says. "Drills are not inexpensive. It takes staff time, and the smaller the community the bigger the drain. Also, if you are really going to run drills effectively you have to run drills that continue to proceed until the system begins to break down. The value of drills is knowing what is not going to work. There is this belief that, 'We ran our drill and everything worked great so it's an A-plus, gold star drill.' It's exactly the opposite. If you run a drill that proves that everything that you are doing is correct you have learned nothing. That is not really a drill."

The guidance document emphasizes the important of drilling collaboratively.

"A lot of times communities drill with the triad of fire, police, and EMS, but they don't drill with their health care infrastructure," he says. "Or often times hospitals drill without the community. There are things learned in doing it that way, but they are not in sync. For community-based drills to be effective all players have to participate. Certainly, one of the key players is the health care system within the community."

The guidance recommends that communities consider such programs as the Community Emergency Response Teams (CERTs). A key component of Citizen Corps, the CERT program trains citizens to be better prepared to respond to emergency situations in their communities. When emergencies occur, CERT members can give critical support to first responders, provide immediate assistance to victims, and organize volunteers at a disaster site. The CERT program is a 20-hour course, typically delivered over a seven-week period by a local government agency, such as the emergency management agency or fire or police department. Training sessions cover disaster preparedness, disaster fire suppression, basic disaster medical operations, light search and rescue, and team operations. The training also includes a disaster simulation in which participants practice skills that they learned in the course.

"There are a number of things that the guide talks about that are available at the federal and state level," he says. "They are well established and communities can plug themselves in. We give them some ideas of how they can be employed in the community plan."

While resources and coordinated training are challenges, there may be a bigger obstacle to preparedness in rural and suburban communities.

"They may have a certain level of complacency," he says. "They are in middle America, a suburb or smaller community. They don't think of themselves as a terrorist target and may have not had weather [related disasters] in a number of years. They are not as tuned in to this as they probably should be. But the idea of planning is not just for a terrorist attack. It can be for anything that could eventually threaten the community – a natural disaster, pandemic flu, whatever. It allows a certain responsiveness for a variety of things."

Finding dual uses for existing or emerging capabilities is also particularly critical for resource-strapped small, rural, and suburban communities. A reverse 911 call system established by a community for law enforcement emergencies could also be used to communicate information about other types of emergencies. Motels and college dormitories can be used for additional bed capacity, the document states. Investments made by local public health departments in upgrading laboratory services for smallpox, severe acute respiratory syndrome, anthrax, and other specialized testing can buttress routine laboratory services in the community. Boats or school buses can provide alternative means of emergency transportation. Businesses with call-center capabilities can support community communication needs during a disaster. 🏠

Lucky 13: Key Steps to Small-town Readiness

A recently published planning document by the Joint Commission on Accreditation of Healthcare Organizations outlines 13 essential components of an effective community-based emergency management planning. Components include:

1. **Define the community**
   - Identify key stakeholders in defining the community.
   - Consider geopolitical and other definitional factors.
   - Consider impact of federal definitions.

2. **Identify and establish the emergency management preparedness and response team**
   - Build on existing relationships.
   - Identify appropriate planning partners.
   - Consider start-up logistics.

3. **Determine the risks and hazards the community faces**
   - Use an "all-hazards approach."
   - Acknowledge the potential for a catastrophic event.
   - Compile a list of potential hazards.
   - Recognize the problems inherent in hazard lists.
   - Assess and prioritize the listed hazards.
   - Fine-tune list by conducting a "gap analysis."

4. **Set goals for preparedness, response planning**
   - Ensure that planning covers basic societal functions.
   - Make the planning process as doable as possible.
   - Address the four phases of emergency management.
   - Address human resources requirements.
   - Plan for convergent responders.
   - Involve the public in community preparedness efforts.
   - Enable people to care for themselves.
   - Plan for layered preparedness and response.

5. Determine current capacities and capabilities

- Use federal government asset categories and target capabilities as a guide.
- Specifically consider the public as an asset category.
- Consider other groups not yet represented at the planning table.
- Identify geographic features and vulnerabilities that may affect capabilities.
- Consider surge capacity and consult surge planning resources.
- Consider all community health resources.
- Define critical capacities for each health entity and link to state databases.
- Know the federal government's definition of required surge capacity.
- Consider the issues involved with standards of care during mass casualty events.
- Identify dual uses for existing or merging capabilities.
- Identify alternative care and shelter facilities.
- Identify federal resources in the community.
- Identify gaps in community assets.

6. Develop the integrated plan

- Maintain a collaborative effort; broaden planning partnerships where necessary.
- Choose an approach to developing the plan.
- Use available guidance and resources.
- Determine how the plan is to be drafted and the expected time frame.
- Agree on meeting frequency.
- Review existing plans, laws, and mutual aid agreements.
- Commit to the use of simple language.
- Clearly delineate roles and responsibilities.
- Determine how the plan will be organized.
- Address all types of events and cover all defined goals.
- Specifically address health and medical facility emergency planning.
- Specifically address how to meet needs for pharmaceutical and medical suppliers.

- Identify and address hazards and resources that cross jurisdictions.
- Identify how preparedness and response success will be measured.
- Consider the lessons learned from 9/11.

7. **Ensure thorough communication planning**
    - Understand how communication is transmitted.
    - Plan for alternative and backup communications links and systems.
    - Plan and provide for emergency backup power to communications systems.
    - Ensure interoperability of communications systems.
    - Use available communications planning resources.
    - Review and build on existing communications planning initiatives.
    - Obtain/prepare information for crisis communications.
    - Define emergency communications protocols or procedures.
    - Establish communications credibility with the public.
    - Recognize and plan for the critical role played by media.
    - Identify how every community member can be reached in an emergency.
    - Plan to provide decisional support.
    - Ensure culturally sensitive communication.
    - Use publicly available communications materials.
    - Ensure integration of the local health care organization's communications plans.

8. **Ensure thorough mental health planning**
    - Use available mental health disaster planning resources.
    - Link to pastoral care resources.
    - Consider organizing self-help groups.
    - Link to and know how to access federal and state disaster mental health plans/resources.
    - Recognize and plan for the emotional effect of crises on rescue and health care workers.

9. **Ensure thorough planning related to vulnerable populations**
    - Identify special-needs populations to support effective communication, outreach, and planning.

- Include a cross section of partners in planning and response efforts related to vulnerable populations.
- Consider the unique needs of children.
- Involve the school nurse in emergency preparedness and response.

10. **Identify, cultivate, and sustain funding sources**
    - Proactively pursue funding.
    - Include all planning partners in the funding requests.
    - Consider revenue-raising opportunities.
    - Seek funding collaboratively and regionally.
    - Consider the impact of funding reductions.

11. **Train, exercise, and drill collaboratively**
    - Identify who should be trained and the training needs for each.
    - Ensure competency-based training programs.
    - Identify cross-training opportunities.
    - Consider offering the CERT program.
    - Access other training programs offered through the federal government.
    - Ensure incident command training for appropriate personnel.
    - Recognize drills or exercises as a critical element of the emergency preparedness process.
    - Involve all players in exercises and drills.
    - Be sure to include local businesses in training, exercises, and drills.
    - Access available resources.
    - Practice with other communities.
    - Identify performance measures for drills and exercises.
    - Ensure the realism of drills and exercises.
    - Include alternative care sites, shelters in disaster drills.
    - Activate the emergency plan.

12. **Critique and improve the integrated community plan**
    - Conduct periodic review and reprioritization of possible emergency incidents.
    - Review emergency management plan on an annual basis.
    - Base review on analysis of performance.

- Discuss post-test problems and assign remedial actions.
- Consider obtaining external feedback.
- Review the planning process.

13. **Sustain collaboration, communication, and coordination**
    - Ensure proper documentation and dissemination of plans and supporting information.
    - Establish mechanisms for receiving and reviewing regional, state, and federal plans.
    - Collect and disseminate information about effective models, practices, and lessons learned.
    - Build multilayered relationships and prepare for transitions.
    - Ensure ongoing communication with the public. ⌂

In the ED

Chapter Contents

Evacuate or 'Hunker Down'? ED Experts Ponder Options
As Katrina Wreaks Havoc 45

Staffing up Helps EDs Handle Katrina Surge 49

System Addresses Ability to Transition in Emergencies 53
    • *Patient Readiness Ratings*.. 54

System Came out of 9/11 Response 57

Lessons Learned From Hurricane Katrina: EDs Share
Their Best Disaster Strategies 61

Will You Meet the Needs of ED Nurses During Disasters?..............................65

Katrina-born Tracking Forms Aid Rita Response 69

Triage During a Mass Disaster: The Usual Rules Don't Apply 73

Make Decontamination Part of All-hazards Plan..79

When Disaster Strikes: Treating Patients When Your
Department Shuts Down...81

Space, Staff Key Concerns in ED Surge Capacity Plans...................................85

Hospitals' Preparation for Surge of Patients Helps With
New Joint Commission Standards 87

Evacuate or 'Hunker Down'? ED Experts Ponder Options as Katrina Wreaks Havoc

Hurricane Katrina, clearly, was a health care disaster of unimaginable proportions. Gulf Coast hospital emergency generators were rendered inoperable by rising floodwaters. In many facilities, there was no plumbing or potable water; buckets were used for latrines. In New Orleans, helicopters sent to evacuate critically ill patients were fired upon.

"Many of these hospitals were turned into armed camps; there were nurses and doctors walking around with shotguns slung over their shoulders, and no one questioned it," points out William (Kip) Schumacher, MD, CEO and founder of The Schumacher Group, a Lafayette, LA-based practice management firm that provides emergency medicine, staffing, and practice management services to 104 facilities, including 30 in Louisiana.

No one would seek to minimize the scope of this disaster, and clearly no one questions the dedication and courage of the thousands of emergency medicine professionals who provided whatever help they could under such dire conditions. But those conditions all arose after Katrina hit, and there are those who wonder whether some of the stricken EDs and hospitals – or at least some of their patients – should have been evacuated ahead of time.

There are facilities with such plans in place, and some of these plans have been put into action when disaster seemed imminent; but conversations with a number of ED managers and experts in hurricane-prone areas reveal that to do so would involve a number of key decisions – most of which are never cut and dried.

Not everyone leaves

Even when a pre-evacuation is undertaken, that action does not necessarily mean the facility is entirely deserted, explains Obed Cruz, RN, the ED manager at Mercy Hospital in Miami. Mercy has done partial evacuations.

"There is always a remainder that stays behind, because there are always some patients who can't be evacuated," he says. "Our ED faces the [Biscayne] Bay – so the nearer the storm gets, you literally close it, because the entire site becomes an evacuation area."

This partial evacuation was done in preparation for Hurricane Ivan, he recalls. "Anyone who needs to be admitted [from the ED] quickly goes upstairs,

Chapter 2: In the ED

where beds are available because some other patients have been moved," he says. Any visitor stuck in the ED "becomes part of the family till it's over," adds Cruz, as hurricane shutters in front of the ED are closed.

At St. Joseph's/Candler Health System in Savannah, GA, the facility is considered a community resource in times of disaster, "so [total evacuation] is not a consideration," says Judy Peterman, RN, MSN, director of critical care and emergency services.

"We would discharge all the patients we could and send them elsewhere or manage them in a crisis if need be." With a Category 3 hurricane or higher, they have relationships established with outlying facilities, should they need to transfer ED patients.

When you are hired, you are assigned randomly to Team A or Team B, says Anne Byerly, RN, assistant ED nurse manager for St. Joseph's/Candler. "In the event of a hurricane, Team A stays," she explains. "Team B leaves the city."

Texas Children's Hospital in Houston would evacuate ahead of time. "We know what the ramifications of a Category 4 or 5 would be to Houston," says Mary Frost, RN, trauma coordinator.

"We have a Level 1 center in Galveston that evacuated ahead of time in 1983 for [Hurricane] Alicia, which was a Category 4," she notes.

When do you decide?

The criteria for evacuation and the decision itself should occur well in advance of the anticipated landfall, Cruz notes. "You can't wait until it's almost going to hit," he emphasizes.

The second you are in a hurricane watch, the plans need to already be in place, Cruz advises. "Usually, as soon as a watch has been issued in your area and you are in the path, the handwriting is on the wall and it has to happen pretty quickly."

The most dangerous part in all of this is the dangers on the road, he says.

These dangers can include downed power lines or massive trees falling on vehicles, which, according to a Mercy spokesperson, was the cause of death in the first three Katrina-related fatalities in Florida.

At Mercy, the decision to evacuate is made by the safety officer and hospital administration, Cruz says. What storm category does he believe warrants evacuation? "If it gets to a 3 or 4, you are definitely looking at something that will be pretty devastating," he says.

In New Orleans, however, conditions shifted so rapidly that such advanced evacuations may not have been possible, counters Randy Pilgrim, MD, president and chief medical officer of The Schumacher Group.

"We opened our command center well in advance, but during a 48-hour period, the storm ranged from a 3 to an extremely strong 5, resulting in the fact that all the backup plans and emergency preparedness we had crafted on Saturday had to be completely revisited and re-crafted on Sunday," he says.

On Monday, after the levees in New Orleans broke, the plan had to be so substantially redone that it was unrecognizable, Pilgrim notes. "The point is, when you think about evacuating or closing a hospital, it's extremely difficult to be sufficiently preparatory but not overreactive."

You may not have assurances that evacuating patients won't place their lives at risk, he says.

If evacuation has to occur by helicopter, there is a tremendous risk of helicopter transport itself, including crashing, Pilgrim explains. Under circumstances of wind, rain, and adverse weather conditions, it is even more risky, he says.

"A patient in a room with electricity, oxygen, and all life support is in a very stable environment; if you move them to a vehicle, [intravenous lines] can come out, [endotracheal] tubes can become dislodged from airways," Pilgrim adds. "In the best of hands, in a controlled situation, it generally goes smoothly; but the risks are all that much greater under storm conditions or conditions of relative chaos."

In Cruz's facility, there are several levels of response, and the ED is well prepared to keep operating during the toughest of times.

"We have an option called the 'sheltering in place' plan, where we just weather the storm in the hospital," he explains.

"In the ED, if we have to move to the second floor, everything is wireless, so we could move the entire ED and our computers all the way to the second floor and be able to operate in a matter of two to three hours. If we were hard-wired, there would be a lot of disadvantages," he adds.

Cruz describes the decision to evacuate New Orleans as a tough call. "You're not talking about 100 or 200 patients, but thousands. It's hard to come up with scenarios to manage that kind of disaster, and it's easy to point a finger if you're not in charge."

For more information, contact:

- Anne Byerly, RN, Assistant ED Nurse Manager, St. Joseph's/Candler Health System, 5353 Reynolds St., Savannah, GA 31405. Phone: (912) 819-4300.

- Obed Cruz, RN, ED Manager, Mercy Hospital, 3663 S. Miami Ave., Miami, FL 33133. Phone: (305) 854-4400.

- Mary Frost, RN, Trauma Coordinator, Texas Children's Hospital, 6621 Fannin St., Houston, TX 77030. Phone: (832) 824-1000.

- Judy Peterman, RN, MSN, Director of Critical Care and Emergency Services, St. Joseph's/Candler Health System, 5353 Reynolds St., Savannah, GA 31405. Phone: (912) 819-4300.

- Randy Pilgrim, MD, President and Chief Medical Officer, The Schumacher Group, 200 Corporate Blvd., Suite 201, Lafayette, LA 70508. Phone: (800) 893-9698.

- William (Kip) Schumacher, MD, CEO, The Schumacher Group, 200 Corporate Blvd., Suite 201, Lafayette, LA 70508. Phone: (800) 893-9698.

Staffing up Helps EDs Handle Katrina Surge

Hurricane Katrina's impact was felt far beyond those areas that received the storm's direct fury. From Alabama to Texas, EDs that already were overcrowded had to deal with a sudden influx of transfers that, in most cases, doubled their normal censuses. How were they able to handle this sudden surge of patients? ED managers on the front lines said a combination of good planning, staffing up, and a healthy dose of outside assistance helped them to soar instead of sink.

Chris Ritchey, MD, FAAP, medical director of the children's ED at Women's & Children's Hospital in Lafayette, LA, said the number of patients about doubled. Calls from transferring facilities in the New Orleans area alerted him ahead of time, which was a big help, he said.

"We were able to put all our docs on call, and they came in for extra shifts," Ritchey added. "Nursing was tough for a while, but HCA [Hospital Corp. of America, which owns Ritchey's facility] has really done well getting us staff from other locations."

Anticipating needs is crucial

He also tried to anticipate the kinds of supplies he would need. "We thought we'd see a lot of injuries, cuts, and wounds, so we got extra suture kits and bandages," Ritchey explained. "People were in that water for awhile, so wound infections were a concern. We got extra [intravenous] fluids for dehydration and antibiotics for infection."

One week after the hurricane hit, Summit Hospital in Baton Rouge, LA, still was averaging about 45 patients more than a normal day, which is about 78, says Dave Miller, RN, ED director.

"We had to gear up staffing mainly," he said. "As long as we were staffed well enough, we were able to move patients through pretty quickly."

Miller says he increased his nursing and physician levels by about 35%. "Normally during peak times, we have six nurses, and we were running about nine to 10," he said.

Usually the ED has one physician with a physician assistant (PA) eight hours a day, Miller says. "We went to a PA 24 hours a day and a swing shift with an extra physician," he noted.

Handling 25,000 patients

Surprisingly, the area with the largest influx of new patients seemed to handle them as well if not better than any other relief locale.

Houston took in more than 200,000 evacuees and about 25,000 hospital patients, "but almost all of our hospitals were kept off diversion," asserted Mary Frost, RN, trauma coordinator at Texas Children's Hospital.

The reason was the creation of Houston's Regional Unified Medical Command Center, which was established following the destruction of Hurricane Allison in 2001. "We have coordinated the responses of hospitals," she explained.

Patients were treated at the Astrodome and at the George R. Brown Convention Center. "We were manning some of those ourselves to address pediatric needs," Frost said.

The local medical schools, Baylor and the University of Texas, provided staff at the request of the mayor and the county judge to offer adult care, and they also had out-of-state Disaster Medical Assistance Teams (DMAT) teams.

Patients were first triaged at the Astrodome and then were sent to a shelter, to the on-site clinic at the dome or, if they were sick enough, they were transferred to a hospital, Frost says.

Patients were spread through all the hospitals in the region to keep all the EDs flowing, she continued. "Otherwise, we all would have been on divert."

No hospital, including Texas Children's, had to activate its disaster plan, Frost noted. "And we cared for people [who live] in Houston, plus the additional stress of a holiday weekend, plus our guests from New Orleans."

Many of the patients suffered from chronic illnesses, she said. "We tend to think of injuries when we think of disasters, but we had 10 patients a day coming off the buses needing dialysis. If we hadn't planned ahead and knew who to call, we could never have pulled it off, but we had an organization that was there just to coordinate chronic dialysis."

There is room for improvement – especially in communications, Frost added. They learned a lot about patient tracking, she says.

"Our hospital planning group had some very significant contact with the Red Cross, and they are now another entity within this planning process," Frost pointed out. "We will all have forms for data collection ready for the next time, which were developed on the fly to help us keep track of patients."

Previous hurricane experiences have affected disaster planning in several areas of the country. For example, ED managers at St. Joseph's/Candler Health System in Savannah, GA, have been concerned for some time about their low-lying, waterfront location. Subsequently, they made improvements, says Judy Peterman, RN, MSN, director of critical care and emergency services.

"Generators and backup systems used to be in the basements of both hospitals," she noted. "We have had some near-misses, and they are now on the second floors."

At Texas Children's Hospital, several changes grew out of Hurricane Allison, which hit in 2001 and caused six hospitals to flood, Frost added.

"We understand what New Orleans [flooding] means," she says. "We took from our experience, built on it, and developed relationships we had not had before. Among the changes to the area hospitals themselves were the addition of flood doors," Frost said.

There's no doubt that once you've been through such an experience, you have a totally new perspective on preparation, said Obed Cruz, RN, the ED manager at Mercy Hospital in Miami. He went through an evacuation prior to Hurricane Ivan.

"If I had not gone through one, I'd be just as blissful as anyone else," Cruz conceded.

For more information on handling patient surge during a disaster, contact:

- Dave Miller, RN, ED, Director, Summit Hospital, 17000 Medical Center Drive, Baton Rouge, LA 70816. Phone: (225) 755-4858.

- Chris Ritchey, MD, FAAP, Medical Director, Children's Emergency, Women's & Children's Hospital, 4600 Ambassador Caffrey, Lafayette, LA 70508. Phone: (337) 521-9100.

System Addresses Ability to Transition in Emergencies

A scoring system for assessing which patients are most ready to be discharged from the hospital can be an important emergency preparedness tool, suggests Pat Orchard, CCM, CHE, director of health services for Horizon Blue Cross Blue Shield of New Jersey, based in Mount Laurel.

"It's a methodology for tracking acuity," says Orchard, who has worked as a case manager in a variety of settings. "A lot of organizations have acuity systems but use them for determining nursing staffing ratios – [a defined number of] acute patients to a nurse."

The same concept, she points out, can be extremely valuable when used to determine a patient's readiness to be transferred to the next level of care. Hospitals that categorize patients in some format indicating "readiness to transition," Orchard adds, can move quickly and efficiently in the event of disaster or even ED overcrowding.

"When you're talking about capacity, what comes in must go out," she notes. "The balance has to be there. If not, there's a tremendous amount of delay."

Typically, organizations focus on input – getting ED patients into treatment rooms and then to the nursing floor, for example, Orchard says. "But if you don't address output, managing patients to move them out efficiently and effectively, you don't solve the throughput problem," she points out.

Without a system for categorizing patients, she explains, hospital staff faced with high-capacity moments may spend hours trying to free up beds.

"Say, for example, you had to move 40 people out of the hospital because there was a disaster in the community," Orchard adds. "Nurses are [examining] every patient in the hospital to determine readiness [to move]. Everyone is running in circles trying to find beds."

If a scoring system is in place, however, the patients who are most ready for discharge already will have been identified and – after physician orders are obtained – can be moved quickly and easily, she says.

Step 1: Establish criteria for acuity levels

The first step in implementing such a system is to establish criteria for acuity levels and categorize patients based on those criteria, Orchard advises.

"You can use numbers, or letters, or any kind of scoring you want, but you are scoring the patient based on readiness," she adds.

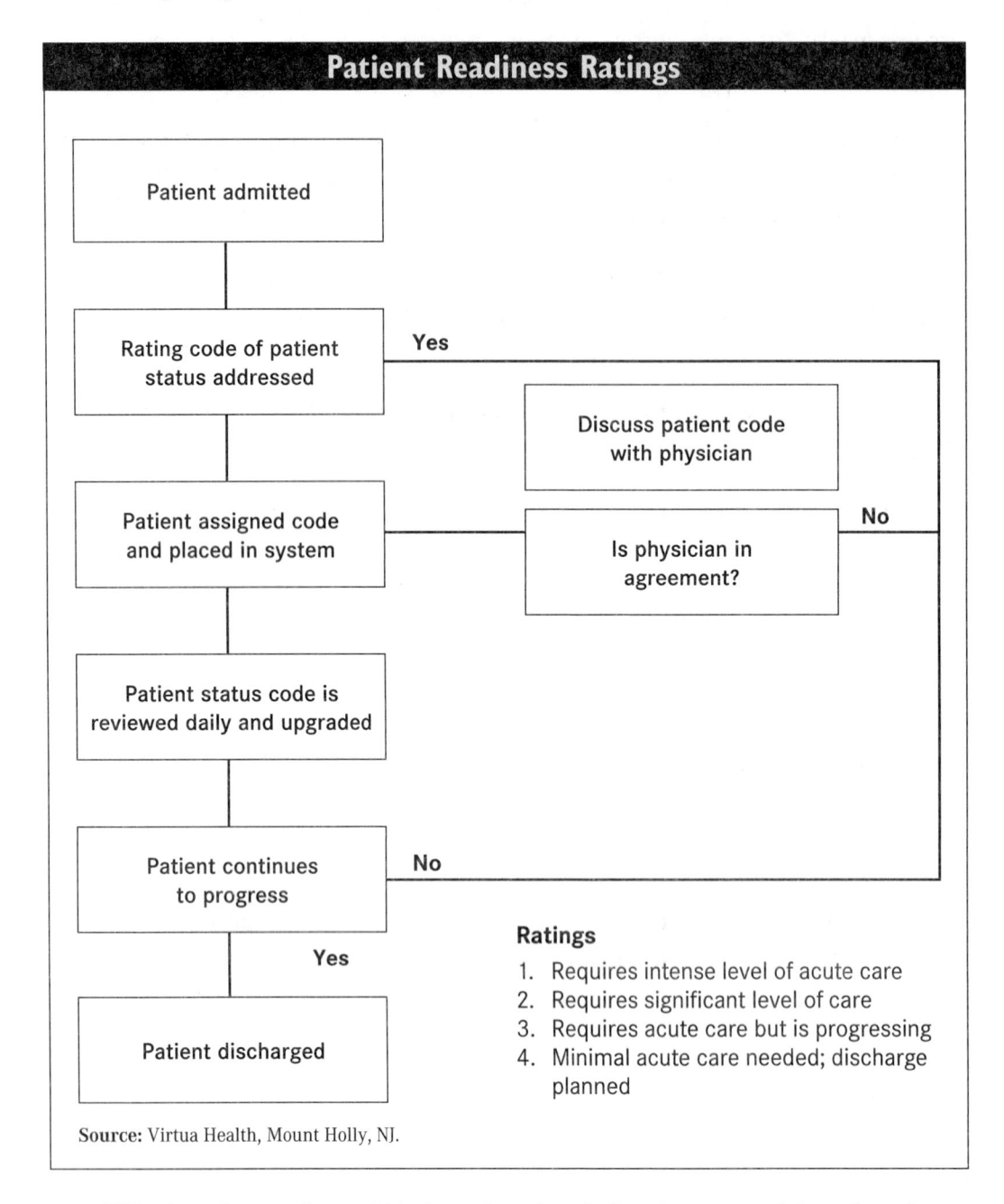

Patient Readiness Ratings

```
Patient admitted
      │
      ▼
Rating code of patient ──Yes──┐
status addressed              │
      │                  Discuss patient code
      │                  with physician
      ▼                       │
Patient assigned code ────────┤              No
and placed in system     Is physician in ────┐
      │                  agreement?          │
      ▼                                      │
Patient status code is                       │
reviewed daily and upgraded                  │
      │                                      │
      ▼                                      │
Patient continues ──No───────────────────────┘
to progress
      │
      ▼ Yes
Patient discharged
```

Ratings
1. Requires intense level of acute care
2. Requires significant level of care
3. Requires acute care but is progressing
4. Minimal acute care needed; discharge planned

Source: Virtua Health, Mount Holly, NJ.

Whether the scoring grid is based on 1 to 4, 1 to 3, or something else, the information can be put into the computer system and pulled out in a report when needed, she says.

"If you're using a score of 1 to 4, those patients who are leaving in the morning, waiting for nursing home placement, or finishing one more course of treatment may be 4s. This is a basic acuity system, but it's based, not on clinical findings, but on the transition capability of the patient," Orchard explains.

"How quickly can they transition to the next level of care?" she asks.

These are patients about whom physicians say, "Maybe they can go tomorrow, or maybe they should stay one more day," Orchard adds. "Some physicians don't move patients as fast as they could."

From a managed care perspective, she says, some might question why such patients still are in the hospital if they can be discharged safely. But the fact is, they are there, she continues.

"Maybe the physician hasn't been in yet, or the physician was in that morning and test results weren't back then. Multiple inefficiencies are out there," Orchard notes.

Once a scoring system is in place, she adds, "at least you know where to focus your attention."

"Have a set of parameters," Orchard suggests, "so that when you do get in a crunch, you're able to turn quickly to the high-level patients who can be moved out immediately. Make sure physicians have agreed to the process and to the scoring system the hospital has developed."

Whether the physician must be called when the process is put in motion – as the result of a crowded ED or a natural disaster – depends on the policies of the organization, she says. "Most would call to get the discharge order."

Assessing and scoring of patients should be done daily or even twice a day, depending on the hospital census, Orchard recommends.

"If done in conjunction with nursing or case management rounds," she adds, "the time required should be minimal."

System Came out of 9/11 Response

Virtua Memorial Hospital, of Burlington County in Mount Holly, NJ, was one of the facilities that got a call on Sept. 11, 2001, asking staff to find room for a possible deluge of patients seriously injured in the attack on the World Trade Center, says Dee Page, RN, director of case management.

"We were one of those hospitals in the Northeast that was in close enough proximity that we thought we would have an influx of patients," she explains. "On Sept. 11, we got a call about 10 a.m. and were told to be ready. At that time, it was thought that we would have a lot of sick and injured patients," Page continues.

By 11:30 a.m., the hospital had emptied 62 beds in preparation for the expected patients, but unfortunately, most of the victims turned out to be casualties, and the beds weren't needed after all, she adds.

The quick and the dirty

That experience, however, led to the development of a quick and dirty way to determine which patients could be moved on a daily basis, she says, not only in the event of an emergency, but to address throughput.

The case management department established a scale of 1 to 4, with 4 being the lowest acuity rating, "the patient closest to the door," for whom there is a discharge plan in place, and 1 indicating an intense level of acute care, Page says. Next are the 2s, who require a significant level of care – patients in a step-down unit or maybe telemetry.

The level 3 patients require acute care but are progressing, she continues. "These may be postoperative patients, or those who are being treated aggressively and showing improvement, but who are not primed enough to go to a skilled nursing facility.

"There could be a fifth tier," Page notes, "a shaded area that would more or less indicate a patient who is being observed. If you wanted to push the envelope, you could add this level."

A departmental flowchart shows each patient and the rating code for the person's status. (See "Patient Readiness Ratings," p. 54.) The patient's readiness level is determined at admission and reassessed daily, she says.

The readiness rating also is entered into a web-based system that includes utilization review and discharge planning information, Page adds. "Pieces of that documentation are printed and placed in the chart, and the rest lives in the system as a lifetime record."

That system is helpful at the time of discharge, she says, because it documents where patients are sent or referred.

"Where we fall short [with the patient readiness rating] is that nursing does not use it with us," Page points out. "The nursing department has not decided to go along with this," she says.

"The nursing department had a readiness project of its own – a color-coded system that was tied to staffing ratios as well as patient acuity," says Page.

"What that meant to them was that, if census and acuity go below certain levels, the staffing is adjusted. As soon as they see the coding, they know they need extra staffing or that there are empty beds.

"The [nursing project] never got off the ground, but we continue to use our system," Page adds. "We know at any time how many beds are occupied by a particular type of patient."

In addition to its value during times of overcrowding or crisis, she notes, the patient readiness score helps caregivers prioritize the workload if a case manager is not there, and take a more proactive role in assisting physicians with discharge decisions.

"In our documentation system, we have an RC [review case] due date," Page explains. "For instance, if you have a managed care patient, and have just done a review with the payer, and the payer authorizes a three-day stay, technically, you wouldn't have to look at [that case] for three days."

System helps prioritize

While that system helps in managing caseloads, she points out, "the readiness rating goes beyond the obligation to see the patient again." There might be six patients on the case manager's list who require acute care and are progressing, Page adds, but the readiness check could reveal that one of those patients is now a 4.

The case manager then can suggest to the physician that the patient might be ready for an earlier discharge, she says. "So it helps them further prioritize – it's very valuable in that respect.

"It used to be that if you knew you were being paid for three days, you left it alone, but we really don't feel that way anymore," Page points out.

"It's better to have your beds filled with people who are really sick. It's better for the patient if you can move beds sooner."

With abdominal surgeries, insurance companies often authorize lengthy stays, and patients may be ready for rehab or discharge sooner, she adds. "The theory of 'Fill your beds, fill your beds' doesn't work anymore."

In terms of the readiness scoring system, the focus of the case manager's day is with the 2s and 3s, Page says.

"With 2s, you want to make sure you can move them through the system to a more appropriate bed, or ask, 'Have they finished that course of treatment? Do they need to be transferred to another facility?'"

With 3s, she adds, the idea is to make sure they are not the next patients to be designated as 4s. With 4s, the discharge plan is complete and just needs to be activated, Page notes. "If someone was told yesterday that [he or she] could move to rehab today, that patient would have been a 4 yesterday."

System not labor-intensive

When the time comes to empty some beds quickly, case management – the only department using the patient readiness system – gets the first call from one of Virtua Memorial's bed-flow coordinators, she says.

"We often go on divert here – beds are full, and we have to send patients elsewhere – and [the coordinator] comes to us right away, asking, 'What can we do to open some beds?'"

When that call comes, Page says, "We go right to the 4s and make some calls to physicians to let them know there is a crunch. Sometimes, they say they're in the hospital and will be up to discharge the patient. They almost always want to see the patient."

With elderly patients who will be transferred to nursing homes, she notes, the case managers often will have gotten a heads-up that, for example, the patient still is receiving treatment, but this will be the last day. In those cases, Page adds, the discharge might be all sealed up for a particular date.

Although the readiness system is an internal mechanism for the case management department at present, Page says she would like to see it fully implemented at all the Virtua Health campuses.

"It's not labor-intensive at all," she notes.

"It's putting a sticker on the chart. On those days when we're short-staffed, or even when we're full and somebody wants to organize the day, it helps to have [the rating].

"Instead of relying on a whole lot of other people for information, the case managers can look at the scale and see what they have, and know which patient to address first," Page adds. ⋔

For more information:

- Pat Orchard, CCM, CHE, Director of Health Services, Horizon Blue Cross Blue Shield of New Jersey in Mount Laurel. E-mail patpj@att.net.
- Dee Page, RN, Director of Case Management. Virtua Memorial Hospital in Mount Holly, NJ. Phone (609) 267-0700.

Lessons Learned From Hurricane Katrina: EDs Share Their Best Disaster Strategies

You may have planned for an influx of injured patients and fine-tuned your decontamination process. But what if your own hospital is flooded, the ED has to be evacuated, and some of your patients are armed and dangerous, with no law enforcement in sight?

That's the situation some ED nurses faced in Louisiana, Mississippi, and Alabama during the aftermath of Hurricane Katrina, and it was a scenario none had addressed in disaster drills. EDs across the country are left asking, "Could we have gotten through it?"

The catastrophic results of the hurricane are incomprehensible, notes Sharon S. Cohen, RN, MSN, CEN, CCRN, clinical nurse specialist for North Broward Hospital District in Fort Lauderdale, FL. "To me, it equates to the tsunami [the Indian Ocean or Asian Tsunami in December 2004]," she says. "Every disaster presents learning opportunities, and we're going to have to learn from this."

Constantly thinking of "what-if" scenarios and incorporating these into disaster drills is of utmost importance, says Cohen. Having a plan in writing means nothing, she says. "Practicing it is the only way to find opportunities to improve," she says. "Every disaster is going to be different, so the more scenarios you practice, the more prepared you are."

To significantly improve your ED's preparedness, do the following:

Don't get caught short-staffed

Previously, North Broward Medical Center divided ED nurses into two groups: those who would work before and during a storm, and those who would work after. This caused a problem during 2004's Hurricane Francis, when the dangerous storm remained overhead for an entire day.

"We discovered that we didn't have enough staff for the before/during phase, which was a huge stress on the 12 nurses we did have," recalls Philip Ragusa, RN, regional manager of emergency services. "They ended up having to work for 36 hours straight."

Now, the ED has a day and night shift for both the "before/during" and "after" groups. "For Katrina, we implemented our disaster mode at 3 p.m., so everybody already at work went home except the before/during day shift, who worked 3 p.m. to 7 a.m., and the before/during night shift who worked 7 a.m. to 7 p.m.," he reports.

Chapter 2: In the ED

Drill on an off shift

The Joint Commission on Accreditation of Healthcare Organizations requires that one of your disaster drills be held during an off shift. "You can have a disaster drill go smooth as silk, but how well prepared will your staff be at 9 p.m. on a Saturday?" asks Ragusa. "The amount of resources available during the off shift, both in terms of manpower and accessible supplies, is very different."

Ask nurses for input

Immediately after a drill is held, or as soon as possible after an actual disaster, North Broward's ED has a post-conference to solicit feedback on what could have been done better, says Ragusa.

"This is a critical component that people often forget about. The best lessons learned come from the people who work at the bedside with the patient," says Cohen, adding that critiques should be done right away. "It may be midnight and staff will want to go home, but if you wait 48 hours, people start forgetting some of the details."

After you obtain feedback, set a timeline of 36 hours to write an "after-action" report listing needed changes, she recommends.

When a disaster drill is scheduled, two ED staff members are asked to be evaluators and are paid overtime for this, says Cohen. "They know what the normal process of the ED is, so they can tell you where the bottlenecks are," she says. "It may be as simple as changing the direction a door opens."

Disaster plans should be revised continually, based on lessons learned from your own drills or actual disasters, says Jeanne Eckes-Roper, RN, director of emergency preparedness for the North Broward Hospital District. They also look to other institutions and their lessons learned, to identify opportunities for them to improve, Eckes-Roper says. "Disaster preparedness is a dynamic process and always will be," she says. "It has to be fluid."

Include decontamination

Even natural disasters can have hazardous components, such as gas, waste products or chemicals, notes Cohen. In New Orleans, there were biohazards floating in the water, she says. "You need always to be thinking, 'Do patients need to be deconned? Do we need to take care of exposure in addition to the injury?'"

A recent disaster drill scenario at North Broward involved a bomb exploding on a train coming from Miami releasing an unknown chemical, so all patients had to be decontaminated. "We included one person with a pre-existing debilitating injury who also had to be decontaminated," recalls Ragusa.

Despite the fact that pre-hospital personnel were told to send all "walking wounded" patients to surrounding hospitals for the drill, there still were a number of patients who walked into the ED themselves, Ragusa notes. "Many people will drive in themselves and need decontamination, so we completely locked down the hospital."

Identify alternate care sites

If your ED is filled to capacity, you may need to care for patients with minor illnesses or injuries in areas such as auditoriums, cafeterias, infusion centers, or outpatient surgery areas, says Eckes-Roper. "As part of their plan, each of our hospitals has identified alternate treatment sites outside their EDs."

During a disaster, Cohen's ED uses an ambulatory clinic as a "mini-ED." "It's not meant for stroke or heart attacks, but we can do wound checks and the things that don't need to be clogging up EDs," she says.

Update call lists

An up-to-date personnel callback roster in the ED will avoid delays when staff members need to come in immediately, and you should review callback lists periodically, says Eckes-Roper. "In addition, every time a storm threatens, the managers are asked to make sure it is up to date," she says.

Whether you contact staff by e-mail, telephones, cell phones, or pagers, you should update your list at least quarterly, says Cohen. "The best way to do this is to drill your callback procedure, for example, the first Monday of every third month," she says. "The more often you update the list, the better prepared you'll be when you need to call in staff during an incident or disaster."

Have backup communication plans

The No. 1 failure of most critical incidents is communication, notes Cohen. "If you are basing your communication on a singular plan, you're going to end up getting caught," she says. "Your backup plan has to have a backup plan."

For example, you need to plan for internal phones being down and your dispatch down, Cohen adds.

Cohen's ED relies on land lines, wireless phones, and two-way radios – and all of these would have failed during Katrina. "The New Orleans EDs lost every known form of communication," Cohen says. "They lost cell phone towers, pretty much anything." With a Category 5 storm, satellite phones are about the only communications tool that works, she adds.

Ham radios also are a possibility when all else fails, says Cohen. "Anytime our mass casualty incident plan is activated, part of our plan is to call one of our volunteers who is a ham radio operator," she notes. ⋔

For more information on disaster preparedness, contact:

- Sharon S. Cohen, RN, MSN,CEN, CCRN, Clinical Nurse Specialist, Emergency Preparedness, North Broward Hospital District, 303 S.E. 17th St., Fort Lauderdale, FL 33316. Phone: (954) 355-5109. Fax: (954) 468-5270. E-mail: sscohen@nbhd.org.

- Jeanne Eckes-Roper, RN, Director of Emergency Preparedness, North Broward Hospital District, 303 S.E. 17th St., Fort Lauderdale, FL 33316. Phone: (954) 712-3931. E-mail: JECKES@nbhd.org.

- Philip Ragusa, RN, MBA, Regional Manager of Emergency Services, North Broward Medical Center, 201 E. Sample Road, Deerfield Beach, FL 33064. Phone: (954) 786-6866. E-mail: pragusa@nbhd.org.

Will You Meet the Needs of ED Nurses During Disasters?

Working days without sleeping or eating, worried about the safety of their own children and family members. These were the horrific conditions ED nurses faced during Hurricane Katrina.

During any disaster, ED nurses may be working short-staffed under dire, chaotic circumstances with inadequate supplies and staff. But what if nurses also haven't eaten or slept in far too long?

"You have to take care of your staff so they can take care of the patients," says Rachelle Zahniser, RN, regional manager of the ED at Coral Springs (FL) Medical Center.

This doesn't happen by accident. It needs to be part of your disaster plan, says Anne Byerly, RN, nurse manager of the ED at Candler Hospital in Savannah, GA. It is obvious from the stories from Hurricane Katrina that ED managers must review policies and discuss all aspects of them, she says.

"As the interim manager of the ED, it is my responsibility to make sure all the needs of the emergency nurses are being met," she says. "This is when administration has to put on those scrubs and join the ED staff."

To ensure that needs of ED nurses are met during disasters, do the following:

Make sure nurses get adequate rest

Before Hurricane Katrina hit, staff were given designated sleep areas and meal times, says Zahniser. "Staff members that were assigned sleeping times during scheduling meetings were excused and would get updates when they were on duty," she says.

"Wake-up call" rounds were done to ensure a smooth transition between shifts by giving staff time to shower and eat beforehand.

"We know when everybody is sleeping and who is responsible for waking them up," says Zahniser. Rest may be limited, but staff aren't working 40 hours without sleep, she says. "That does nobody any good, and you will have a worst-case scenario," she points out.

When Savannah was evacuated during 1999's Hurricane Floyd, nurses who worked in Candler's ED during the storm brought clothing and personal supplies from home and stayed for several days, says Byerly. Several treatment rooms and the day surgery area were used for sleeping and showers, and nurses brought their own food and drinks.

"We slept, ate, and bathed in the hospital," she says.

Bring supplies as needed

At Memorial Health in Savannah, GA, nurses are asked to bring the following items to the ED during disasters: flashlight with extra batteries, bottled water, snacks, pillows, sleeping bags, clean clothing, personal hygiene items, and personal medications.

Although the hospital has enough supplies for staff and patients for 72 hours, additional patients may be picked up after the storm when search and rescue begins, says Debra O'Connor, RN, senior nurse for the ED.

"The staff may want some snacks, and the supplies don't allow for food to be left out and wasted," O'Connor says. "The other suggested personal supplies are a good backup if there is a delay in relief arriving."

Decide whether to allow family members

During Katrina, many ED managers allowed staff to bring in family members and even pets. "Allowing family members might prove to be a burden to the ED," says Zahniser. "Ideally, you want the least number of people in the hospital. Otherwise, you become inundated."

The ED asks nurses to complete forms requesting to bring family members in during disasters, and cases are individually reviewed, she explains.

Staff are advised to make plans for their family in the event of an evacuation or disaster, taking into consideration special needs such as age or disabilities. The "B" team is released from the hospital 18 hours prior to the storm arrival. Candler's updated policy states that the hospital cannot accommodate family members, so staff must make provisions for family prior to evacuation.

However, during Hurricane Floyd, families were allowed to accompany staff at Candler's ED, but they had to provide their own food and drinks. "In fact, you often saw family members helping to deliver food to the floors," says Byerly. "They also assisted staff to feed and accommodate citizens with special needs who were being boarded in the hospital."

Chapter 2: In the ED

For more information on the needs of ED nurses during disasters, contact:

- Anne Byerly, RN, Nurse Manager, Emergency Department, Candler Hospital, 5353 Reynolds St., Savannah, GA. Phone: (912) 819-8224. E-mail: byerlya@sjchs.org.

- Debra O'Connor, RN, Senior Nurse, Emergency Department, Memorial Health, 4700 Waters Ave., Savannah, GA 31404. Phone: (912) 350-9748. E-mail: oconnde1@memorialhealth.com.

- Rachelle Zahniser, RN, Regional Manager, Emergency Department, Coral Springs Medical Center, 3000 Coral Hills Drive, Coral Springs, FL 33065. Phone: (954) 344-3017. E-mail: rzahniser@nbhd.org.

Katrina-born Tracking Forms Aid Rita Response

Necessity, they say, is the mother of invention, and it can't get much more necessary than trying to track several thousand patients who've suddenly been transferred to your city. That's precisely the challenge that faced the city of Houston in the wake of Hurricane Katrina.

The invention of the trauma professionals who had to face this challenge was a patient tracking form developed "on the fly" and later formalized and modified prior to the arrival of Hurricane Rita.

"If you have been displaced from your home state, your family is going to be looking for you," says Lori Upton, RN, assistant director for emergency services at Texas Children's Hospital and current chair of the area's regional bioterrorism task force. In addition, she notes, it was critical to track patients' movements from one facility to another and to share the information with organizations such as the American Red Cross and with local authorities. *(Editor's note: The U.S. Department of Health and Human Services has made exceptions to the HIPAA privacy regulations for facilities responding to disasters. For a copy of their special bulletin on this subject go to www.hhs.gov/ocr/hipaa, and click on "Hurricane Katrina Bulletin: Disclosing PHI in Emergency Situations.")*

"We were moving patients in and out by rickshaw, by ambulance, by aircraft," recalls Mary Frost, RN, trauma coordinator at Texas Children's. "We even had information on a patient who was put on a C-130 prior to the storm."

The forms started as rough notations on pieces of paper, but "that began to become unruly," says Frost. "We set up an Excel spreadsheet with the patient's name, age, and, of course, everybody was from New Orleans."

She and Upton ended up with 5,000 names, but the original form could be searched only alphabetically.

They then began collecting data from other hospitals on patients they were seeing and shared that information with the aforementioned organizations. "We started to fax and e-mail information back and forth," recalls Frost. "The problem was that everybody had a little different format and take on how to send the information."

Chapter 2: In the ED

Disaster Medical Unified Command/Federal Emergency Management Agency Rita Ambulance Dispatch

Date: _____ Time: _____

Hospital Site: _____

Patient Name: _____

DOB: _____

Chief Complaint: _____

_____

_____

_____

                        Ground   Air

Dispatch to: _____

Notified by: _____

Source: Texas Children's Hospital, Houston.

Preparing for Rita

After the Katrina crisis had subsided (but before Rita's arrival), the two decided to create one centralized type of form for patient information. (See form on p. 70.) It included the patient's name, date of birth, shelter or location they were coming from, chief complaint, the type of transportation that was needed, where they were going to, and who took the call.

"All of that was entered into a database that a biostatistician from the health department developed," says Upton. "With that, we were able to search by name or key data element – hospital, city, 'transported to,' and so forth – to find our patients. If you typed in a last name, you could go back and find these people for folks calling in, or for the Red Cross."

"That unruly spreadsheet was now searchable," says Frost, and it wasn't any too soon. "Into a system already bursting at the seams from Katrina, [with Rita's approach] we had hospitals in various stages of opening and closing," she says.

There were fewer hospitals, and some of them could offer only limited services, Frost says. "And for Rita, we had people coming from many different places."

They started coordinating nine counties, and it grew to 30, including parts of Louisiana, Upton says. "At first, nine hospitals had to be evacuated, but we ended up with 19 that had to be evacuated," she says. This took 19 facilities out of the search capacity queue, which had been 96, Upton says. "We lost a level 3 trauma center and numerous community hospitals," she says.

The new forms worked much better, says Frost, but she and Upton still are not satisfied. What they want now is a statewide tracking system, she shares. "We realized a disaster like this may not affect just your area," Frost says. For example, they were sending people to Austin, Dallas, and El Paso. "This way, we can continue tracking patients wherever they are sent," she says.

Frost says there's no reason EDs in other cities can't do what she and Upton have done, but they shouldn't assume the same exact forms will work just as well.

"Everybody needs to customize the form for what they want to accomplish," she says.

Every day during Hurricane Rita their mission would change, and they noted it on a white board behind them, Frost says. One day that mission might be the evacuation of a hospital; the next day, it might be nursing homes, Upton says. "What you would end up with was multiple manifests and a summary sheet over it," she says.

Whatever the challenges, the new form proved successful. "We coordinated care for 2,400 patients," says Frost. "In the end, there were only two requests we could not find on our end, and we had not coordinated them."

For more information on patient tracking forms, contact:

- Lori Upton, RN, Assistant Director, Emergency Services, Texas Children's Hospital, Houston, TX. Phone: (832) 824-1000.
- Mary Frost, RN, Trauma Coordinator, Texas Children's Hospital, Houston, TX. Phone: (832) 824-1000.

Triage During a Mass Disaster: The Usual Rules Don't Apply

A catastrophic disaster, either natural or manmade, that not only results in widespread casualties but also wipes out medical resources can force health care providers to abandon typical delivery of care and shift to a kind of battlefield medicine, where the sickest patients may not be treated so that care can be delivered to more.

That's the kind of decisions physicians were forced to make when they were trapped in hospitals in New Orleans after Hurricane Katrina with very sick, frail patients, no electricity, and few medical supplies.

"Doctors and nurses who stayed behind were scrambling to find drugs for their critically ill patients," says Joe Cappiello, vice president for accreditation field operations at the Joint Commission on Accreditation of Healthcare Organizations (JCAHO), who toured New Orleans in the wake of Hurricane Katrina. "[Health care providers in New Orleans] had to make choices that we ordinarily don't make in America, to help those with the greatest chance of survival."

Triage in a typical U.S. hospital on an average, non-disastrous day typically consists of identifying the sickest or most critically injured patients and getting them appropriate care as quickly as possible, perhaps temporarily bypassing patients who are less sick or injured.

That kind of triage has to fall by the wayside to some extent when casualties are many and supplies and physicians are few, according to bioethicist John Moskop, PhD, professor of medical humanities and director of the Bioethics Center of University Health Systems of Eastern Carolina in Greenville, NC.

"There's a whole spectrum of situations that involve what we call triage, and it goes from the sort of routine triage that would happen in any busy emergency department, where we determine how quickly patients need to be treated, whether they can wait or have an urgent need for treatment. At the other end of the spectrum," he explains, "would be a massive disaster, [such as] a nuclear attack, in which many people say triage would be useless, because so many resources would have been destroyed and so many thousands of serious injuries that you couldn't do anything."

But in between are disaster scenarios ranging from multivehicle car crashes that tax hospital emergency departments, plane crashes with hundreds of casualties, battlefield triage during war, or natural disasters like the tsunami that hit Sri Lanka in December 2004 or the hurricanes that hit the Gulf Coast in the late summer of 2005.

"Each one is different; each has different criteria and difficulties for the triage officers, and there are underlying moral criteria involved. These are not typical situations, so there are some departures and some differences from the choices we might make outside a disaster situation," Moskop says.

Outside a disaster situation, when a patient presents to an emergency department with serious injuries, the medical staff do what they can to save the patient. In a large-scale disaster, that person might not be treated – and might die – since diverting the resources and manpower and time necessary to treat him or her might cost the lives or functionality of several more patients who could have been helped in the meantime and who might be more apt to survive.

"It's not an easy thing for people to do, because we don't want to feel like we're leaving someone to die," says Moskop. "One way to defend it would be to say 'This is an extraordinary circumstance, and look at the number we can save, and we're going to save as many people as possible.' And if that means setting another [less salvageable patient] aside, that's justifiable in these situations."

Cappiello, in comments made to the media during and after his visit to New Orleans after Hurricane Katrina, recounted harrowing details of how doctors and nurses felt compelled to ignore the fundamentals of their training and make triage-style choices to aid some patients at the expense of others.

Howard R. Epstein, MD, medical director of care management and palliative care at Regions Hospital in St. Paul, MN, has studied the ethics of triage, and says disasters such as the Gulf Coast hurricanes, bioterrorist attacks, and the Sept. 11, 2001, terrorist attacks have caused physicians to give thought to situations many never thought they would experience.

He says large-scale disasters creating multitudes of casualties require physicians to treat patients based on the concept of medical utility rather than how they treat patients under normal circumstances.

Epstein says hospitalists and emergency medicine physicians who train for disasters should not concern themselves just with the medical aspects of such a frightful scenario.

"We must also prepare ourselves for the real and significant ethical and moral dilemmas we will encounter," when and if they are forced to deliver care primarily to those who benefit most from the fewest resources, he cautions.

Jeffrey Orledge, MD, is an emergency medicine physician at the Medical College of Georgia in Augusta, and is a member of the Georgia-4 Disaster Medical Assistance team that went to Louisiana to assist after Hurricane Katrina. He says even though he has trained in and taught lifesaving and mass casualty triage and was part of the 9/11 medical response to New York the situation demanded he adapt to what he found.

"I was doing triage the first day at the [New Orleans International] airport, and even though I teach BDLS/ADLS and have done the MASS triage station and helped teach that station, I still had to change because of the circumstances," he says. "There were tough questions – chest pain in a patient with a history of cardiac disease having the same type of chest pain, who after one nitro is pain-free, is he a red or green patient?"

In some ways, Orledge says, his decisions may have been easier than those made by hospital-based physicians in a disaster, because what he could offer patients was limited.

"At least we were part of a DMAT team, and we truly did not have enough resources there to do what is normally done, which is 'everything for everybody,'" he says. "That made it easier for me, because we knew our limited resources. I think it would be more difficult in a hospital setting."

"We need to have a conversation about what we would do if, like the doctors at Charity [Hospital in New Orleans], we are put into an ethics situation and have to decide what's right and wrong," says Epstein. "We need to give doctors and hospitals more of an ethical framework, to say that when we impose our hospital's disaster alert, what our medical response is going to be and what our ethical response is going to be."

By and large, Epstein says, physicians are not prepared to make those decisions without some authority from their states or communities that gives them permission to "change the paradigm."

No room for patient autonomy

A prize cornerstone of American health care, patient autonomy, by necessity, falls victim to the pursuit of the greater good when disasters strike, Epstein and Moskop point out.

"Patient autonomy kind of disappears in a triage situation," Moskop says. "That's another way our moral priorities shift."

Chapter 2: In the ED

Epstein says that in a disaster, doing what's best for the individual patient is supplanted by "society's competing interest."

"We are used to our paradigm, but what we're talking about is giving up patient autonomy and saying society has a competing interest," he says. "In a disaster with mass casualties, the balance shifts from individual autonomy to the greater good."

Key to making that shift, Epstein says, is hammering out a framework long before disasters strike, so that the medical staff, support staff, and the community know what health care will look like in a disaster.

"You need to have community support ahead of time, because you don't have the luxury of time to get everyone around a table [during a mass casualty incident]," he says. "You need to prepare in advance and have a plan that's transparent to the community, because if you're going to say 'I'm going to treat this person and not your grandmother,' you need to have already had that discussion and know, as a community, how you're going to handle it."

Moskop says physicians have to realize that even with a plan and set criteria in hand, the disaster and its scope will dictate many of the decisions that must be made.

"Each triage officer has to make tough judgments, such as whether or not a person's injuries justify priority for lifesaving intervention or should be passed over to give the time and resources to someone with a better chance at survival," he says.

Criteria have been developed for triaging patients in a disaster, in an effort to make as many decisions as routine as possible. Those are somewhat successful, Moskop continues, but don't remove all discretion and responsibility from the person making triage decisions.

"And in a situation like Katrina, other choices, like who to transport or not, don't come into play because you're stuck, at least temporarily, with limited resources – the hospitals were not functioning well, were low on supplies, no electricity," he says. "Physicians had to make do with what they had, and there's no way you can plan in that kind of detail."

But ethical issues probably should not arise during the application of disaster triage criteria, Moskop says; ideally, at that point, the physician should be trained and know the criteria, and thus be able to apply them "and not stew over the ethical issues."

"The ethical issues are more in how to design the criteria and deciding who do we give priority to," he explains.

This can include deciding priority – which can mean giving first priority to immediate lifesaving, second priority to those needing urgent but not lifesaving care, then those with minor injuries, and last, those who are so severely injured that they stand little chance of survival. That last group of patients, many say bluntly, may have to be considered a waste of scarce resources.

"Not everyone agrees with that," Moskop points out. "Some people say you should try to give everyone an equal chance to survive, and then, even if most of them die, you can say, 'At least they had the chance.' But I think the majority reject that, and say that in extraordinary circumstances, you have to adopt a different moral perspective given the huge need that we have and the limited resources we have to address that need."

There is another priority advocated by some, taken from the military medicine practice of treating those lightly wounded in battle first, so they can return to the fight. In the case of a disaster in which medical personnel are among those injured, Moskop says an argument can be made to treat them first, so they can then assist in treating the rest of the sick and injured.

Epstein says that even physicians trained in disaster response and mass casualty triage can feel the effects of their decisions long after the disaster has passed.

"We're used to making the best decisions for our own patients and being the best advocates for those patients, regardless of what's going on, but in a triage situation like that, you have to treat those who have the most chance of survival," he says. "I don't think most health care providers are equipped emotionally and ethically, when they're put in a difficult situation, to avoid having ramifications down the road.

"I mean, how much more can you play God than when you say, 'I'm not going to feed this patient so I can feed that one,' or 'I am taking the ventilator off this patient so that I can put it on that patient'?"

Part of an institution's plan for coping with disasters should be provisions for debriefing and psychological counseling, he says.

"Especially if they inflict death on people who haven't asked them to do that," he says. "How do you make that decision at the point of care? There has to be some support [for the practitioner]."

Despite the daunting example provided by Hurricane Katrina and its effects on hospitals in New Orleans, Epstein says he has heard very little discussion among his colleagues at Regions Hospital about how they might respond if put in a similar situation.

"We have medical triage, but there's no way [in place] to make decisions in any fashion other than what we have now, which is the sickest get help first," he says. ■

For more information, contact:

- John Moskop, PhD, Professor of Medical Humanities and Director of The Bioethics Center, The Brody School of Medicine at East Carolina University, Greenville, NC 27858. Phone: (252) 744-2361.

- Howard R. Epstein, MD, Medical Director, Care Management and Palliative Care, Regions Hospital, 640 Jackson St., St. Paul, MN. Phone: (651) 254-3456.

- Jeffrey Orledge, MD, Emergency Medicine Physician, Medical College of Georgia, 1120 15th Street, Augusta, GA 30912. Phone: (706) 721-0211.

- Joseph L. Cappiello, Vice President for Accreditation Field Operations, Joint Commission on Accreditation of Healthcare Organizations, One Renaissance Blvd., Oakbrook Terrace, IL 60181. Phone: (630) 792-5757. E-mail: jcappiello@jcaho.org.

Make Decontamination Part of All-hazards Plan

In the wake of hurricanes Katrina and Rita, health care professionals across the country are revisiting their disaster preparedness plans. And in light of a survey by the Centers for Disease Control and Prevention (CDC), it couldn't be soon enough – particularly in the areas of decontamination preparedness and participation in community planning, which are especially important to ED managers.

The survey, "Bioterrorism and Mass Casualty Preparedness in Hospitals: United States," 2003, was conducted by the CDC's National Center for Health Statistics, and it had responses from roughly 500 hospitals regarding their preparedness for treating patients. Among the findings:

- While 97.3% of hospitals responding addressed natural disasters in their plans, only 85.5% addressed chemical terrorism, 84.8% addressed biological terrorism, and 77.2% addressed nuclear or radiological terrorism.

- While almost all hospitals (95.4%) had provisions in their plans to contact outside entities, only 76.4% defined their role in communitywide planning with other health care facilities.

Don't limit your vision

In revising your disaster response plan, it's critical for ED managers to think creatively when it comes to these key issues, experts say.

"What we want to get across is that you should have an all-hazards plan – whether it's a manmade disaster with political intent, an industrial accident, or a natural event," says Eric Weinstein, MD, FACEP, an attending physician at Colleton Medical Center in Walterboro, SC, and immediate past chair of the disaster medicine section for the American College of Emergency Physicians. If you have too many plans, you're not going to have the right plan, Weinstein says. "If you are good in your daily operations concerning what could possibly happen in a risk analysis of your community, you could pretty much change to adapt to the situation," he says.

And it's in that risk analysis that you've got to think outside the box, advises Kathy J. Rinnert, MD, MPH, assistant professor at the division of emergency medicine at the University of Texas Southwestern Medical Center in Dallas. "You need an all-hazards response regardless," she says, noting that any event might contain a decontamination element.

A bomb blast, for example, might appear at first to involve only blast injuries, but what if the bomb contained biological material? Or, you might have a laboratory blow up, Rinnert says. "You don't only need to know about potential injuries. Responders don't want to get certain chemicals on them."

In doing your risk analysis, creating "wild scenarios" is essential, she says. "A wild scenario on decontamination might be an event that required a certain number of your area hospitals close to new patients and be designated as decon and triage facilities – that's all they do – and the rest of the area's patients are sent on to other hospitals that are 'clean,'" she suggests. "But can you name a hospital that wants to be known as a triage/decon hospital? And you have to have closed hospitals willing to accept inpatients from those facilities."

Sometimes thinking "small" is actually the more creative way to address decontamination considerations, Weinstein adds. "Most of the time, all you really need is a fire truck with an inch and a half spray, and you will pretty much get what you need off [the patients]."

You could work out an agreement with your local fire department to send a truck, or you could go to a local store and purchase polyvinyl chloride (PVC) pipe and some nozzles to use outside your ED, Weinstein says. "People who have stuff on their skin that's stinging them and whose eyes are burning are not going to want to go calmly through a nice, orderly decontamination line," he says.

It's equally important to remember you are not alone, Rinnert says. You must start with a written plan and well-trained staff, but what happens if you haven't worked with other hospitals and agencies, she asks.

"If you don't develop contingency plans, what happens when all your planning assumptions prove inadequate – when your plan is out the door and doesn't apply any more?" Rinnert says.

That's why it's imperative you develop those important relationships before disaster strikes, she says. For example, she says, what if your municipal fire department can't get to your hospital because they are occupied elsewhere? "How about getting a volunteer fire department to come and set up decon?" she suggests. "That depends on you having a memorandum of understanding written ahead of time."

That's exactly what Rinnert has done with the volunteer fire department in a small, nearby town. "You can't call a stranger out of the blue and say you need them to come out and spray people," she says. "They have to already be a good friend of yours."

Chapter 2: In the ED

When Disaster Strikes: Treating Patients When Your Department Shuts Down

You really couldn't blame the folks in Punta Gorda, FL. After all, they expected Hurricane Charley to hit Tampa. Nevertheless, when a surprise right turn put Charlotte Regional Medical Center directly in the storm's path, the ED was as well prepared as it could have been under the circumstances. "We actually had a hurricane drill just a month before the storm hit, which was one of the reasons we were so successful," says Mata Guttman, RN, lead supervisor.

During that drill, significant flaws in the plan were noted and corrected, including finding a new location for psychiatric patients who had to be evacuated and backing up all records for a newly purchased X-ray computer.

Nevertheless, administrators and staff had short notice and a unique situation after learning Charley had changed direction, says Derrell Billington, DO, FACEP, medical director of the ED.

"We probably had three hours before it actually hit, maybe only one hour before tropical storm-force winds hit, and we still had about 75 patients in the hospital – 10 in critical care," he says.

The hospital hurricane plan called for moving the ED to the second floor in case of flooding. "The plan was that we would actually close [the ED] during the storm, but open space on the second floor for people to come to after that," Guttman adds.

They took whatever supplies they could carry or cart up and moved all the patients to that floor, Billington recalls. "The third floor was for family that employees had brought to the hospital," he adds.

All of this movement was done very methodically. The least unstable patients were moved first (the ED had 12 beds), which left the critical ventilated patients for last. "The last thing was to move the ER staff upstairs," Guttman says. "We figured we needed them to the very last minute."

For the patients who were placed upstairs, there was a full complement of staff; and as patients moved, the nurses assigned to them went with them, she explains.

Even the best-laid plans, however, must sometimes adjust to the fury of Mother Nature. "We knew as soon as the brunt of the storm passed over us that we had to evacuate the hospital," Billington explains. "Most of the windows, even on the second floor, were blowing out on us. We had patients in the rooms, so we had to evacuate them into the halls while windows were exploding and glass was flying."

After the patients were moved to the hallways, three male staff members put mattresses against the windows to protect against flying glass, but "you could see parts of the roof fly off," he recalls.

Once the winds began to damage the hospital, the order to evacuate the facility was given, and family members on the third floor were advised to leave, Billington adds. The staff members were reunited with their family once all patients were transferred to other facilities.

Although it was clear the hospital needed to be evacuated, it was easier said than done. Five area EMS facilities were damaged or destroyed, and its headquarters was no longer functional.

"EMS stops running and bridges close down if winds are more than 45 miles per hour anyway, so we had no ambulance services," Billington notes. "It took the hospital 24 hours to completely evacuate."

And even though "we knew we could actually die in the storm," in his words, patients already in the ED, as well as new walk-ins, had to be cared for. "We had a lot of people walking or driving up," he says. "They started to show up rather quickly right after the storm came through."

At first, they were sent up to the second floor, but the hallways soon became too crowded.

"We had to make a decision about where to hold these people coming off the street," Billington recalls. "We didn't know the structural integrity of the building, but finally we decided because of the great number of people looking for treatment, we'd move down to the first floor," which had not flooded.

The ED filled quickly. Some small children had to lie on counters due to the lack of beds and space, and ultimately the cafeteria, next to the ED, was transformed into a triage area, where the walking wounded could be treated and laceration centers set up. Food services kept working and provided a limited menu of sandwiches and water because power was limited.

"We discharged some patients if they had a way to go home once we knew we were under an evacuation order, or quickly made them admissions and moved them into an admitted bed," Billington explains. "The admitted patients had to ride out the storm with us, after which they were transferred."

During this period, conditions remained far from ideal. "When we moved back downstairs, a lot of ceilings had caved in, there was water on the floor, and half the ED did not have emergency power," he says. "In some cases, we had to put people in dark rooms."

Staff had to determine which parts of the hospital had emergency power to run extension cords to hook up fans, lights, and other equipment, Billington adds. Housekeeping proved invaluable in clearing debris, moving cafeteria tables out to make room for hospital beds, and mopping the floors to prevent additional injury from slips and falls.

How did staff handle triage and treatment of the 40 or so patients who came in? "You focus on life and limb," he points out. "We had no EMS, no communications, no X-ray."

Most of the injuries were soft tissue and orthopedic, although there were amputated fingers and one patient whose leg had nearly been amputated through an injury.

"You use your trauma basics: We stopped hemorrhaging, used splints, tried to maintain neurovascular status, and gave a lot of antibiotics and used a lot of narcotics," Billington adds.

What can ED managers facing disasters learn from the experiences of Charlotte Regional?

"You have to be able to make decisions very rapidly, and they had to change rapidly," he says.

In retrospect, Billington adds, your leadership team in the ED should try to meet with the entire staff every hour or two for updates and change direction as your resources change or improve, he says. Communication is difficult in such situations, he concedes, but when decisions are made – such as opening the cafeteria to patients – the word must get out.

"You could even set a time, like meeting every hour on the hour," Billington suggests. "It also would have been nice to have some radio contact, even handhelds." Disaster response can be very dependent on inexpensive devices: two-way radios for hospital staff, flashlights, batteries, battery-powered radios, and TVs.

Anticipating post-disaster injuries is critical, adds Billington. "We knew we had to have lot of antibiotics, narcotics, and splinting material to handle the influx," he says.

Billington concedes, however, that some things are very hard to plan for. "We had an internal disaster as well as an external one," he notes, referring to the damage to the hospital building. "All the disaster plans I've seen have been one or the other, but not both."

In disaster planning, it's important to anticipate many different scenarios, particularly disasters that might hit your specific area, he notes. "Also, we all underestimate the lack of services we will have in times like these," Billington says. "We think we will always have electricity, water, be able to flush toilets, and to clean up after a disaster." Because these facilities did not always work, housekeeping was a crucial part of a successful response, he says.

Finally, Guttman recommends you do a drill every year and plan what you will do with the staff, in terms of protecting and helping them.

"After worrying about how to service the community, you have to worry about how to keep the staff mentally and physically healthy," Guttman says. In the case of Charlotte Regional, that help was provided after the hurricane hit on a Friday in the form of in-house psychiatric staff and counselors.

"Beginning Monday morning, our behavioral center staff positioned themselves, along with our pastoral care persons, in our chapel and ED to provide help to staff and their families," she recounts. "In addition, FEMA [the Federal Emergency Management Agency] had behavioral personnel assisting throughout the county."

Space, Staff Key Concerns in ED Surge Capacity Plans

One of the key challenges for ED managers when faced with a community-wide health crisis – be it terrorism, infectious disease, or natural disaster – is surge capacity.

While such events affect the entire community, "I think it's fair to say the main concern [of the ED manager] should be focused on health care facility surge," says Dan Hanfling, MD, FACEP, director of emergency management and disaster medicine at Inova Health System in Falls Church, VA. "In this day and age with EDs teeming to the brim, [the challenge is] how they can make space available for more patients coming in or an onslaught of patients that just keep coming."

ED managers must ask themselves what actions they should take if they become overloaded, says John L. Hick, MD, medical director for emergency preparedness at Hennepin County Medical Center in Minneapolis. "Do we have an agreement in place for transfer plans to put triage in the cafeteria?" he asks. "Are our clinics available to handle additional patients?"

Making space available is the No. 1 priority, adds Hanfling. "ED overcrowding is more a function of hospital overcrowding, so the hospitals needs to do a better job of expediting discharge," he says.

In the past, Hanfling has used a large patient lobby area as a discharge center, and he is engaged in discussions to use a large corporate building that is across from his hospital because it has a huge cafeteria.

Adjusting triage protocols also can help free more space, he says. "If you canvass your existing ED population and apply a re-triage of patients, you probably will be able to delay or offset a number of those patients presenting for care in anticipation of victims coming from the disaster," Hanfling explains. "You also can cancel elective surgeries, which will make beds available to move ED patients up and out."

Work on life-threatening situations, Hick advises, likening the situation to having to treat a patient in the back of a pickup truck – where an entirely different kind of triage is required. "Ask yourself, 'Do I really need to do this right now?'" he advises.

These situations make clinicians think hard, Hick continues. Ask, "Is this somebody I would normally do, but maybe not now?" he says. You may alter your assessment protocols, Hick says. "With a wound patient, you may watch them with hourly clinical exams rather than doing a [CT] scan," he notes.

To help make these decisions, he adds, there should be a triage gatekeeper – usually the ED manager or head physician.

To make more staff available, you must figure out how to become more flexible and to draw on existing staff or other professionals in the community, Hanfling advises. "You need to get a good sense of what available personnel resources you have; how many docs and nurses can you call back to assist, and how many off-service or subspecialty providers you can rely on," he adds.

Larger facilities will have an easier time filling this staffing need, Hanfling notes, but in any event, it should be addressed in pre-planning. "Concomitant with this is how to alert and notify these people that they may be required," he explains.

In the pre-event planning phase, Hanfling advises, work hard to obtain buy-in for participation, making it clear you will need more doctors and nurses to meet the surge in demand. "Once the event has occurred, your request for support can be done electronically – for example, using page alert phone systems and through local media requests on public channels."

Adequate supplies also should be a major concern, Hick says. "The ER is pretty unique; it's at the hub of a lot of different spokes," he explains. "You need to plan with central supply and other units."

For example, he adds, if you have five chest tube trays, which is an adequate supply under normal circumstances, it would be inadequate in terms of surge capacity. "We had eight handy in central supply, but we upped it to over 25 trays, and 100 suture trays," Hick says. "This is the kind of thing you should worry about."

In terms of the pharmacy, "It's guaranteed you are going to need more morphine," he says, adding that many hospitals do not have enough, even though it is relatively inexpensive. Hick also recommends stocking up on tetanus boosters, midazolam, penicillin, and lorazepam.

Finally, Hanfling advises, be sure to focus on protecting your facility and your staff. "Don't get to where you are so overrun that you put your staff or the patients in your charge at risk," he warns. Personal protective equipment, if required for infection control, is critical. "If you lose the protection required, you can forget about taking care of patients," Hanfling concludes.

Hospitals' Preparation for Surge of Patients Helps With New Joint Commission Standards

With new surge capacity standards from the Joint Commission on Accreditation of Healthcare Organizations, EDs are finding that their preparation for any type of patient surge translates into preparation for the infectious patients specifically targeted in the new standard (IC.6.10), which says, "As part of emergency management activities, the organization prepares to respond to an influx, or the risk of an influx, of infectious patients."

Baptist Hospital of Miami has developed guidelines for a surge of any type of patients, including infectious patients, that allow it to decompress the excess volume in the ED or empty the ED.

Baptist has had to decompress twice, due to the volume of flu cases and other patients, about two weeks apart in March 2005. In each of two situations, more than 20 patients in the ED were admitted and awaiting inpatient beds.

Baptist Hospital identified rooms that were slightly larger than the standard ones, says Becky Montesino, RN, MS, assistant vice president at Baptist. Two patients at a time are moved temporarily to one of these single rooms, Montesino says.

Patients are carefully selected to be temporary roommates in one of these rooms, she says. "We matched for age group, diagnosis, preferred language – general compatibility," Montesino says.

Both patients had to be agreeable, she explains. "Those two patients are just happy to be in a room with a bathroom. Their care is progressing in a safer, much more private environment for them."

As private rooms open on the floors, ED patients are put on stretchers and admitted. "We happened to have electric stretchers in storage for outpatient areas," Montesino says. "We put them into use."

Baptist administrators learned lessons to prepare them for future ED surges. One was that they needed to adjust their computerized billing system so that it could bill for two patients in a private room, as well as scan orders and order meals.

"A surge still requires the same standard of care for everyone," says Montesino, referring to a Joint Commission leadership standard.

Baptist created imaginary room numbers for the patients who were doubled up in a room. For example, if the last actual room on a floor was 2235, a patient admitted to a room with two stretchers would be assigned the room number of 2236.

Other hospitals address this problem by adding "A" or "B," or "Bed 1" or "Bed 2" to the room number.

Baptist also arranged to have second call lights for those rooms. "Now we have them stored and ready to go," Montesino explains. The hospital put tracks in the room to hang curtains as dividers, and they also are stored.

"Planning it before we ever tried it didn't work," she notes. "We learned by experience."

Communicate with all departments

How you communicate changes made during a surge is significantly important, Montesino says. For example, the pharmacy needs to know where to deliver drugs to patients who aren't listed with their actual room number, she says.

E-mails are sent to the directors of every department when implementation of the surge capacity plan seems imminent, Montesino says. Every department has a role, she adds. A meeting is called for the director of every department. The directors are told that the patients are surging, and the changes to normal policies are explained. Directors are asked whether they need anything to help them handle the surge. "From that point out, every department knows how to handle it," Montesino says. For example, the dietary department staff understand that there would be two trays going to some rooms.

Additionally, signs are posted on every unit informing physicians that due to high patient volume, some patients are being admitted on stretchers. They are informed to check with the charge nurse at the desk to find out where their patients are located. "We knew they would get confused," Montesino notes.

Baptist learned an immediate good lesson. "You need to communicate with the patients before they go into that setting," she says. "Be direct and honest about the situation."

Undo the double rooms as soon as you can, she advises. "You don't want to get stuck," she says. "It's an emergency."

After weathering the two surges earlier in 2005, the administrators realized that these changes would help address the new surge capacity standards.

"After we debriefed on these guidelines, we determined with our infection control director that we could use this same method and expand on it as need be," if there was a surge of infectious patients, Montesino says. "We had developed a system that worked already," she adds. "Every nursing care unit understood it."

One area that isn't addressed in the current surge guidelines is the additional staff that would be needed in the event of a disaster or an infection. "We have a pool, and we have some ways to do that because we have to stretch staff in disasters, like Hurricane Andrew in 1992," Montesino explains.

Hospital drafts response policy

St. Joseph Medical Center in Towson, MD, has drafted a surge capacity response policy that could be used in the event of a surge of patients, infectious or otherwise.

"When the Joint Commission was here, they were informed of the draft and what we were doing for surge and how functionalities change as we need to for census management," says Carole Mays, MS, RN, CEN, director of emergency services.

The ED has experienced surges during flu seasons and at other times, Mays says.

"We decided to be proactive," she says. The policy involves all departments, Mays emphasizes. For example, housekeeping is involved in cleaning beds in the ED and on the floor, she says.

"We make sure we decrease and increase staffing, as we need to switch capacity changes," Mays notes.

The ED already has a clinical placement nurse to address capacity issues, she says. Bed meetings are held twice at day, at 8:30 a.m. and 4 p.m., every day, regardless of the census, Mays says.

All the patient care coordinators/clinical leaders attend, plus housekeeping. The ED is represented by the patient care coordinators, the manager, or Mays. "We say, 'We're on diversion' or not, so we let whole hospitals know at that time what our needs are," she adds.

The leaders discuss how many patients in the ED are admitted and don't have beds, Mays says. "Also, we let them know what our potential admissions are. In essence, the hospital helps respond to us by pulling patients from the ED."

When facing surges, the hospital expects physicians to make their rounds differently, Mays notes. Case managers call them, she says.

Also, "They are notified at some of their ground rounds and in the physician lounge that we're in a surge time and we need beds for admissions," Mays explains.

Physicians are asked to assist by rounding earlier and by helping patients understand when they'll be discharged. Case managers are asked to help with the transportation needs of discharged patients, Mays says. "It's a whole effort," she points out.

Other ideas that aren't yet part of the written surge capacity plan include bringing a phlebotomist from the lab to the ED and having physicians at triage to help plan care, May says.

"It's important to us to keep our doors open – our ambulatory doors and our ambulance doors," she says.

For more information on the surge capacity standards, contact:

- Carole Mays, MS, RN, CEN, Director of Emergency Services, St. Joseph Medical Center, 7601 Osler Drive, Towson, MD 21204. Phone: (410) 337-1543. E-mail: carolemays@chi-east.org.

- Becky Montesino, RN, MS, Assistant Vice President, Baptist Hospital of Miami, 8900 N. Kendall Drive, Miami, FL 33176. Phone: (786) 596-6556. E-mail: beckym@baptisthealth.net.

Coping With Disaster

Chapter Contents

Infection Control 101 for Temporary Shelters 93

Shelter From the Storm: ICPs – A Voice of Reason in
A Mind-numbing Disaster 99

Failure to Provide Backup Power Results in Death
And a $450,000 Massachusetts Settlement... 105

Larger Role in Disaster Planning Seen for Quality Managers 111

Health Care Heroes Weather Gulf Storm with Guts and
Emergency Planning 115

Chief Nursing Officer Recounts Katrina Efforts 119

Case Managers Face Challenges of Hurricane Katrina 123

Case Study: Pensacola Hospital and Patients Survive
Battering by Hurricane Ivan... 127

Florida Managers Deal with the Effects of
Back-to-back Hurricanes.. 131

Chapter 3: Coping With Disaster

Infection Control 101 for Temporary Shelters

In the wake of Hurricane Katrina, the Centers for Disease Control and Prevention recommends the following basic infection control measures to prevent transmission of infectious diseases in temporary community evacuation centers:

Infection prevention for residential evacuation centers

Use of appropriate infection prevention measures by all staff and evacuees can reduce the spread of infectious diseases.

1. Staff and residents should wash their hands with soap and water often.
2. Children should be assisted in washing their hands with soap and water frequently.
3. Alcohol hand gels are an effective addition to hand washing, and a reasonable temporary substitute when soap and clean water are not readily available.
4. Alcohol hand gel should be positioned throughout the evacuation center, especially at the beginning of food service lines and outside of toilet facilities.
5. Encourage good personal hygiene practices including the following:
   - Cover your cough with tissues, disposing of tissues in the trash, or with your hands. Wash your hands or use alcohol hand gel after coughing. If possible, tissues should be provided in evacuation center living areas.
   - Follow good hygienic practices during food preparation.
   - Do not share eating utensils or drinking containers.
   - Do not share personal care items such as combs, razors, toothbrushes, or towels with any one else.
6. Facilities should be adequate to allow residents to bathe at least twice weekly.
7. Laundry facilities should be available to allow appropriate laundering of clothes and bed linens.

Hand hygiene

After an emergency, it can be difficult to find running water. However, it is still important to wash your hands to avoid illness. It is best to wash your hands with soap and water, but when water isn't available, you can use alcohol hand gel made for cleaning hands. Here are some tips for washing your hands with soap and water and with alcohol hand gel:

When should you wash your hands or use an alcohol hand gel?

1. Before eating food.
2. After handling uncooked foods, particularly raw meat, poultry, or fish.*
3. After going to the bathroom.
4. After changing a diaper or cleaning up a child who has gone to the bathroom.
5. Before and after tending to someone who is sick.
6. Before and after treating a cut or wound.
7. After blowing your nose, coughing, or sneezing.
8. After handling an animal or animal waste.
9. After handling garbage.

*Food handlers should wash hands with soap and water before beginning work and before returning to work from any toilet visit or break. Alcohol hand gel should not be substituted for food handlers.

Cleaning the living area

Keeping surfaces and items clean helps to reduce the spread of infections to residents and staff.

1. Clean surfaces with a household detergent when visibly dirty and on a regular schedule:
   - Kitchens and bathrooms should be cleaned daily and as necessary.
   - Living areas should be cleaned at least weekly and more often if necessary.
   - Bed frames, mattresses, and pillows should be cleaned/laundered between occupants.
   - Other furniture should be cleaned weekly and as needed.
   - Spills should be cleaned up immediately.

2. Sanitize (i.e., reduce microbial contamination to safer levels) high-risk surfaces using a household disinfectant (e.g., a product with a label stating that it is a sanitizer) or a mixture of 1 teaspoon of household bleach in 1 quart of clean water (mixed fresh daily). High-risk surfaces include:
   - Food preparation surfaces.
   - Surfaces used for diaper changing.
   - Surfaces soiled with body fluid (e.g., vomitus, blood, feces).

Laundry

1. Garments heavily soiled with stool should be handled carefully, wearing gloves, and placed in a plastic bag for disposal. If stool can easily be removed using toilet paper, the garment may be laundered as described below.
2. Wash clothing in a washing machine using normal temperature settings and laundry detergent.
3. Household bleach can be used in the rinse water at normal concentrations.
4. Dry clothes in a dryer, if possible.
5. There is no need to disinfect the tubs of washers or tumblers of dryers if cycles are run until they are completed.
6. Make sure donated clothing is washed before distribution.

Garbage

1. Waste disposal should comply with local requirements including disposal of regulated medical waste such as syringes and needles.
2. Facilities should provide for proper disposal of syringes and needles used for medications. Containers designed for sharp waste disposal should be placed where sharp items are used. A heavy plastic laundry detergent bottle with a lid may be used if official sharps containers are not available.
3. Use trash receptacles lined with plastic bags that can be securely tied shut.
4. Trash bags should not be overfilled.
5. Place trash in an area separated from the living spaces, preferably in trash bins.
6. Have waste pickups scheduled frequently – daily, if possible.
7. Separate medical waste from household waste for pickup; follow local guidelines for pickup of medical waste.

Special considerations for nonresidential evacuation centers

Nonresidential evacuation centers such as stadiums and churches have limited capacity for providing sanitary and food preparation facilities. Bathing and laundry resources also are likely to be limited. In general, it is preferable for nonresidential facilities to only be used for very short-term evacuation. Food service and laundry should be provided from external sources rather than attempting to set up poorly controlled on-site alternatives or allowing residents to attempt these activities individually.

Because of the potentially high ratio of residents to toilets, nonresidential facilities have a particular need for frequent and supervised cleaning and maintenance of sanitary facilities. Designated evacuation center personnel should staff each restroom, controlling the number of individuals using the facility at one time, ensuring that surfaces are wiped down with disinfectant at least hourly, and that basic supplies such as hand soap, paper towels, and toilet paper are maintained.

The ability to clean surfaces in nonresidential settings may be limited by the size or other physical characteristics of the facility. This increases the importance of hand hygiene. However, such facilities also are likely to have limited availability of hand washing sinks. Thus, additional attention should be paid to positioning alcohol hand gel dispensers in convenient locations throughout the living areas and at the beginning of food-service lines, and ensuring that all arriving residents are instructed on their use and availability.

Open sleeping areas should be set up to prevent crowding, ideally with at least 3 feet separating each cot from the next.

Management of people with infectious diseases in evacuation centers

The arrival of evacuees who may have open wounds, symptomatic infections, and unrecognized or incubating infectious diseases, combined with potential for crowding and limited sanitary infrastructure, increases the risk of infections spreading among residents and between residents and staff. In particular, respiratory infections, diarrheal diseases, and skin infections or infestations are prone to spread under these conditions.

Before entering an evacuation center, all residents should be screened for these conditions:

1. Fever
2. Cough
3. Skin rash or sores
4. Open wounds
5. Vomiting
6. Diarrhea

People with any of the above conditions should be admitted to the evacuation center only after appropriate medical evaluation and care. Residents of the center should be instructed to report any of the above conditions to the center staff. If a potentially infectious condition is identified in a person already residing at the evacuation center, the ill individual(s) should be separated from other residents or transferred to a special-needs evacuation center.

A separate area or room should be identified in advance to be used to house potentially infectious residents awaiting evaluation or transfer. If several residents with similar symptoms are identified, they may be housed together in one area. However, cots still should be separated by at least 3 feet.

A dedicated restroom should be identified if possible and reserved for use of the ill individuals only. More than one separate area may be needed if more than one illness is identified in the population, e.g., an area for people with diarrhea and another area for people with a cough and fever.

Such separate areas will need to have extra staff members dedicated to monitoring people housed there and ensuring that the area is kept clean and appropriately supplied.

Source: Centers for Disease Control and Prevention, Atlanta

Shelter From the Storm: ICPs – A Voice Of Reason in a Mind-numbing Disaster

An infection control professional, attorney, and Louisiana native, Julie Savoy, BSN, RN, JD, brings a unique perspective to the horror that was Hurricane Katrina. But first and foremost, in the chaotic first days of the disaster aftermath in New Orleans, she was just another worried relative trying to reach loved ones and offer shelter from the storm.

Her aunt and uncle, both 79, had lived in New Orleans for 55 years. Savoy's mother urged her brother and his wife to leave, but having weathered two previous hurricanes, they decided to hunker down and face Katrina. Foolhardy in hindsight, their decision actually didn't look that bad shortly after the massive storm made landfall and passed through the area. The house still was standing, high and dry.

"About 9 a.m. Monday morning [Aug. 28, 2005], my uncle called to say they had lost power but the house was fine and it look[ed] like the worst is over," says Savoy, an attorney at Gachassin Law Firm in Lafayette, LA.

"Then he said, 'The water is starting to come up fast in the streets; let me go.' And that was the last we heard of them. They were in the area where the Industrial Canal levee broke. We didn't hear from them until Wednesday, a little over 48 hours later, when my uncle called to say they had arrived at a shelter in Baton Rouge," Savoy adds.

What happened in the interim was straight out of the newscasts of house floods, attic sanctuaries, and rooftop rescues. Sometimes, it is difficult to appreciate the forces of nature except through direct experience. Savoy's uncle for one, said before the storm that the wood was so hard in his sturdy old house it was difficult to even hammer a nail into it. "He said the force of that flood water just knocked the baseboards off the walls," Savoy says. "That was pretty impressive to me. They got up in the attic and lived up for there for two days."

The house took on 5 feet of water in about 20 minutes, but the attic remained dry and the resourceful couple managed to save some food and water. "They were never in real danger of drowning," Savoy notes. "It was just surviving until they could get rescued."

A next-door neighbor flagged down a helicopter from his rooftop, and when the rescue team picked him up, they left a crew member to check on Savoy's aunt and uncle. "My uncle felt good about that because he knew they would come back to get that crew member," she adds. "The chopper came back and lowered the basket for my aunt. My uncle had to carry her out of the attic and get her in the basket."

Savoy's mother went to Baton Rouge to find her kin at a shelter, but was told they had already been triaged and dispatched out to an unknown location within the city. After hours of searching, she found them and took them back to her home in Lafayette that night. "This is her only family; she was definitely going to get to them," Savoy continues. "I think a small part of her wanted to give her brother a piece of her mind about not evacuating."

There would be plenty of time for admonitions, but first the stubborn uncle was taken to a clinic. It seems the flood-soaked attic ladder broke out from under him on one of the trips up and down for supplies. "It splintered and ripped up his legs," Savoy explains.

"The minute I heard that, that's when my infection control mind kicked in. The first thing I thought of was *Vibrio vulnificus*. He already had some cellulitis setting in, but it wasn't *Vibrio*. We got him a tetanus shot and an antibiotic. Luckily, it resolved," she adds.

ICP's instincts on target

Savoy's instincts were right on target at the time the Centers for Disease Control and Prevention (CDC) had identified at least 22 cases of *Vibrio* – including five that were fatal.

The infection typically is acquired through shellfish consumption but can be acquired directly from water contact via open wounds. *V. vulnificus* does not spread from person to person.

It primarily is a threat to the immune-compromised, capable of causing acute illness within one to three days of exposure.

The incubation period can be as long as seven days for some cases. Signs and symptoms include fever, swelling and redness of skin on arms or legs, blood-tinged blisters, low blood pressure, and shock.

"If you are in contaminated water and you have cuts or abrasions or some sort of break in the skin, the bugs get in and establish a local infection that may not be very prominent," says William Schaffner, MD, chairman of the department of preventive medicine at Vanderbilt University in Nashville, TN.

"It may not create a whole lot of pus, but then it gets into the bloodstream, and that's very likely what happened with these cases," he explains.

The situation was exacerbated considerably when the national broadcast media began describing the infections as "cholera-like," which was inevitably shortened simply to cholera: a nasty, potentially fatal enteric infection that has rarely appeared in industrialized nations for more than a century. The symptoms of cholera are profuse watery diarrhea, vomiting, cramps, and low-grade fever.

"This, of course, was nonsense. It was *Vibrio vulnificus*," says Schaffner, who asked the media department at his hospital to call the television network and report the error.

The confusion apparently began because the pathogen is something of a second cousin to cholera's etiologic agent, *Vibrio cholerae*, he explains.

As counterintuitive as it seems, the widespread perception of imminent disease outbreaks following hurricanes is not well founded in science. For example, decaying bodies create very little risk for major disease outbreaks, particularly from agents not already endemic to the geographic area.

"Disasters do not bring in new infectious agents," Schaffner says. "They just expose people to the agents that were already there. Outbreaks of infectious diseases are not common after floods or, for that matter, after volcano eruptions. We are always worried about it, but they are not. That's just a fact. We can take some comfort in that."

That said, there will be some very real infection control concerns in the weeks and months ahead. ICPs warning about outbreaks in the crowded shelter conditions found they were being heard – for a change – loud and clear.

"It was amazing to me to see the physicians talk first and foremost about their concerns about disease control," Savoy says. "It's gratifying for me to see that. They get it. Even though in the hospital setting, day to day, the ICPs have their struggles with compliance."

An outbreak of norovirus, the bane of cruise ships, hit evacuees gathered in Houston's Astrodome. Some 700 people were treated, with 40 placed in isolation cohorts to contain the virus.

"After norovirus, I would worry about the enteroviruses echo and coxsackie because these are the viruses that go around in the summer time," Schaffner notes. "There is, undoubtedly, hepatitis A in the sewers of New Orleans, and so there was some exposure. Everybody is concerned about that, and indeed the CDC is now recommending that people who are in congregate settings get hepatitis A vaccine."

'Don't be mesmerized by the hype'

In the meantime, evacuees were reporting to emergency departments and being hospitalized for all manner of illnesses. Schaffner urges that ICPs insist standard protocols for incoming patients are applied, even though infection fears, both legitimate and absurd, have been whipped into a frenzy.

"Use standard routine infection control practices for all of the usual indications," he emphasizes. "Standard precautions with isolation indications as usual. These people are not pariahs. We don't have to do anything unusual. If these evacuees come to your institution, treat them in the standard way. Don't be mesmerized by the hype that's on TV. The little bit extra they will probably have to do is provide education and reassurance to their colleagues in the hospital. They may have unreasonable anxieties."

If nothing else, one infectious disease threat may prepare us for the next. For example, common sense respiratory etiquette precautions adopted during the global SARS outbreak still are in effect at the emergency department and waiting areas at RHD Memorial Hospital in Dallas. "We never really removed respiratory etiquette," says Patti Grant, RN, BSN, MS, CIC, director of infection control. "We still have the respiratory etiquette in place, and anything else would be covered by standard precautions."

Thus, even as thousands of evacuees came into the Dallas-Forth Worth area, Grant was confident that her routine infection control measures would hold the day. "Not being in a flood area or an area that was geographically hit by Katrina, our emergency room situation is more in control here," she says. "We do get patients every day, some of them coming from the shelters, some who have relocated with friends and family."

However, one key difference is that the health department asked city hospitals to switch to active surveillance, routinely reporting each morning the type of conditions being seen in both routine patients and evacuees.

"Pretty much from Sept. 1 forward, we went from passive to active surveillance," she says. "Every day, by 10 in the morning, there are two forms that need to be faxed into the county. They are not just gathering information on victims of Katrina, but they are also wanting real-time reporting of things we normally only report once a week."

The concern is palpable, but thus far infectious disease problems have been minimal. "We have been very fortunate here," Grant says. "It was odd to listen to the news as everything was transpiring and hear words like cholera and typhoid almost instantaneously. I was very proud to be a member of a profession that immediately jumped on that and said, 'Wait a minute; these diseases are not even endemic to our area. They are not going to just pop up out of the middle of nowhere.'"

The nightmare stories

As an employee of a Tenet hospital, the chain that owns five hospitals in New Orleans, Grant spent some volunteer hours working the phone lines and talking to beleaguered health care workers from that hospital and other facilities.

"I can't believe the stories I have heard," she says. "I worked several volunteer hours on the Tenet health line for the employees. People just really want to talk. One called me from a Wal-Mart. It looks like most health care workers truly tried to evacuate as many people as they could."

Savoy adds, "The stories I hear coming out of those [swamped hospitals] are just horrific: having to let patients go because they couldn't continue to bag [manually ventilate] them. You can only continue to do that for so long. It is very difficult on the staff. The nurses and staff were starting IVs on each other to rehydrate themselves because they didn't have food and water," she notes.

While full-blown investigations and newly formed commissions will work to uncover what went wrong and why, Savoy says essentially the hospitals were not prepared for the levees to break.

"They fully expected the buildings themselves to withstand the storms, and they had their emergency provisions," she says. "I think people forget that this was really two separate catastrophic events. The flood that occurred on Monday night was not anticipated. It completely blocked off access to those facilities – the generators were flooding out and then they ended up without power. That was something that was never planned for."

The liability claims, medical malpractice, and wrongful death suits eventually will hit like a second storm surge, she says. "I don't think juries are going to be very forgiving of facilities that may not have had adequate plans to address the issue," Savoy adds. "But I think individual providers who did the best they could within the circumstances will probably fare better in terms of liability."

And what of Savoy's aunt and uncle who so fiercely resisted leaving their beloved New Orleans? "They bought a car and a house here," she adds. "They're not going back."

Failure to Provide Backup Power Results In Death and a $450,000 Massachusetts Settlement

News: A retired polio survivor, who was medically dependent upon a negative pressure breathing jacket and a biPAP machine, shared a room in a nursing home with her spouse. During a power outage, the facility's emergency generators failed to operate. Without electricity for her medical device, the nursing home resident went into respiratory distress. There was confusion about her do-not-resuscitate order (DNR) and cardiopulmonary resuscitation (CPR) was not immediately administered. She was placed on life support and transported to a hospital where she died shortly after the ventilator was removed.

Background: The 72-year-old retiree and her spouse shared a room in a nursing home. She had survived polio and suffered from several associated disabilities and medical conditions that required constant supervision. She could breathe on her own while awake, but needed the breathing apparati while she slept. The machinery consisted of a negative-pressure breathing jacket (NPJ), which was a partial body suit, and a biPAP machine; both were electricity dependent.

Three months after moving into the nursing facility, two power outages occurred. The first happened during an afternoon and the emergency generator immediately came on and functioned properly. The second outage was at night and the generator failed. The NPJ and biPAP machine were plugged into a special outlet that was supposed to, but did not, receive emergency power. The elderly woman went into respiratory distress and became unresponsive. Due to her DNR, there was confusion among the facility's personnel as to what to do, and CPR was not administered until the decedent's husband revoked the DNR. She was placed on life support and transported to the hospital. The next day, the ventilator was removed and she died.

The plaintiff claimed that the defendant nursing home was negligent in failing to provide reliable emergency power for the medically necessary life support system. The defendant countered that the power failure was beyond its control. The plaintiff also faulted the facility for delaying the administration of CPR under the unusual and extraordinary circumstances that caused her to go into respiratory arrest. A $450,000 settlement was reached prior to trial.

What this means to you: The review of this case is significant for risk managers who are plagued by weather concerns – possibly associated with hurricane and tornado season – worried about national security, or followed Terri Schiavo's case.

Depending upon where you are in the country, power outages may be common, routine, or rare. Their occurrence may vary by the time of year. For instance, the Midwestern and Northern states may have an increased risk for power outages in the wintertime in conjunction with heavy snow and/or ice storms. In the South, the onset of summer thunderstorms often is associated with outages. And some, like the 2003 grid failure in the Northeast, just happen.

"Regardless of the time of year or cause of the power outage, facilities should, to the best of their abilities, make appropriate allowances and contingency plans for patients who are dependent upon medically essential electric-powered equipment," says Jay Wolfson, DrPH, JD, distinguished service professor for public health and medicine at the University of South Florida in Tampa, and the appointed guardian ad litem for Terri Schiavo.

"Facilities are also advised to review and know the status of the law in their backyard for, in some jurisdictions, the liability for the interruption of electric services – regardless of the reason for the outage (including nonpayment of the electric bill) – is statutorily assigned to the utility customer and ultimate responsibility is placed on the utility customer for any backup equipment or power supply. This potentially takes the utility companies out of the liability loop, and in this case, the utility customer would likely have been considered the nursing home as opposed to the resident," he notes.

Depending upon the jurisdiction, there may also be statutory requirements placed on health care facilities over and above that of other utility customers to provide backup power, such as a requirement to have a generator.

"Even if there are no statutory requirements placed on nursing homes or health care facilities to provide backup medical equipment and/or electricity, an inventory of residents or patients that are dependent upon electric-powered equipment would have been helpful under the circumstances described in the case. Such a list would have provided staff with a prioritized list for triage, transport, and treatment as necessary. If the staff at this particular nursing home had a list of patients who were energy-dependent, someone might have known that simply waking up the patient may have saved her life. Unfortunately, staff arrived too late and [were] unsure about what to do under the circumstances," Wolfson explains.

While the case appears to be one of a routine or normal power outage, liability issues may be different in cases where the power outage is associated with a declared state of emergency.

"Liability rules change with the advent of a state of emergency and had that been the circumstance giving rise to the power outage in the case presented, the facility may have fallen under limited immunity under the premise that the outage was not only out of its control but out of any entity's control. This may not have had any affect on the nursing home's responsibility for its residents. However, it may mitigate the liability associated with new arrivals and victims of the state of emergency. For the standard of care may be different for those already entrusted to your care as opposed to those seeking care out of necessity," he says.

"Follow one of the credos of risk managers: What is the worst-case scenario? Keep in mind the Sept. 11 terrorist attacks, local weather patterns associated with various seasons, and events such as earthquakes and how they might play out in your community and for your particular institutions and organizations. Risk managers should become familiar with state laws and regulations and even local ordinances that may relate to such disasters – before they occur. This may also give rise to your review of force majeure or Act of God contract clauses with utility providers and other contractors upon whom you might rely for various services – particularly essential services. The language in those contracts can help to identify problems beyond the reasonable control of the parties to an agreement that will excuse performance of the terms of the agreement. You may want to tie your performance under such circumstances to that of your contracted services, so that the other party is required to perform to the extent that you remain in operation," Wolfson advises.

"Disasters and weather aside, health care facilities are bound to follow the health care decisions and directives made by their patients, and if the facility is unable to do so for whatever reason, then the patient should be transferred or assistance should be given to help resolve the matter. Of course, this presumes that contingency plans have been designed," he adds.

Following this case example, upon admission to a health care facility, one of the key questions is whether you have a DNR, and this question often is followed by whether or not the patient has a living will, health surrogate or other health decision makers. While both are indicative of health care decisions, the two instruments are very different. A DNR is a physician order advising that, in the event the patient goes into either cardiac or respiratory arrest, no CPR should be given to the patient. Medical personnel including emergency medical technicians, paramedics, hospital emergency services, nursing homes, assisted living facilities, home health agencies, hospices, and adult family care centers may honor a properly executed DNR order. And, absent a visible or known DNR order, every person and patient is presumed to consent to CPR.

But be aware of your state laws. In some jurisdictions, for the DNR order to be valid it must be on a specific form adopted for use in that particular jurisdiction. Many states will not honor a DNR executed in another state. In addition, the form must be signed by the patient's physician and by the patient or if the patient is incapacitated, the patient's health care surrogate, proxy, attorney in fact under a durable power of attorney, or court-appointed guardian. The form and format of the DNR is different from a living will in that a physician signs the form but it is not otherwise witnessed and as such does not constitute an advance health care directive.

"Even if the DNR is properly executed, valid, and visible, it may only allow for the possibility of the withholding or withdrawal of CPR. This allows the health care practitioner some latitude to make a judgment call in light of the prevailing circumstances, which is important for, as noted, some jurisdictions do not allow the DNR form to be customized," Wolfson explains.

"Most persons executing a DNR arguably believe or assume that they are doing so that, in the event they experience cardiac or respiratory arrest as a result of the normal course of nature, CPR will not be administered. This would not reasonably include the failure in an institution's power backup system. While it appears from the facts presented, the power outage was not intentional and may have occurred naturally, it may not have been a cause of arrest contemplated by the woman or her spouse. We do not know from the facts presented what the staff really thought about her condition when they arrived on the scene. Staff may have believed that it was too late to administer meaningful CPR and stood behind the DNR as much as matter of the medical circumstances at the time of arrival opposed to the unexpected reason for the respiratory arrest. It does appear that there was some discussion of the matter between the spouse and staff, but ultimately the spouse withdrew the order, though we don't know how long it took for him to do so. The bottom line is that a jury may be comfortable viewing the circumstance as something that could have been prevented," he adds.

Living wills differ from DNRs. Living wills and advance health care directives are the result of landmark legislation. Congress was urged to take action in light of the tragic case of accident victim Nancy Cruzan. Her parents fought and eventually gained the right to make end-of-life decisions on her behalf. The Patient Self-Determination Act of 1990 allows competent persons to make binding, legal decisions about their health care preferences, including the ability to withhold life-prolonging procedures. In turn, most states have enacted advanced health care directives legislation and most will honor the directives produced in compliance with the other jurisdictions.

"Following the experience with the Schiavo case, living wills with greater, rather than lesser, specificity are encouraged. For example, they should state whether or not antibiotics or therapy for newly diagnosed conditions should be initiated, withdrawn or avoided in the first place. And clear reference should probably be made to initiation and/or termination of artificial support systems including respirators, feeding and hydration tubes," Wolfson warns.

Health care surrogates are separate from, but should be used in conjunction with, a living will. The surrogate creates the equivalent of a power of attorney for the making of health care decisions. It delegates to a specific individual the legal authority to make either general or limited, specific decisions about a person's health and medical care. Its form may vary across jurisdictions, but it generally requires witnessed and notarized signatures. The nexus of the living will and the health care surrogate occur when the surrogate moves to initiate, discontinue or not receive medical interventions in order to execute the intentions of the living will.

"While not highlighted but certainly noted in the case was the decision to withdraw life support from the patient. We are not told if the decision was made pursuant to a living will or by her spouse as a health care surrogate, but it appears to be an uncontested decision. And, too, once the ventilator was detached, the patient died and the subsequent decision to administer any further life-prolonging procedures such as hydration and/or sustenance did not need to be made," Wolfson notes.

"This case is unlike the more recent case of note involving the decision to withdraw life-prolonging procedures, which was, and still is to some extent, the hotly contested, debated, and publicized case of Terri Schiavo. Ms. Schiavo did not have a written living will or a health care surrogate, and her parents vehemently disagreed with the decision made by the patient's husband who was also her court-appointed guardian. Ms. Schiavo survived the removal of a ventilator following cardiac arrest and a coma, and was able to breathe on her own, unlike the polio survivor who had been dependent upon breathing apparati for most of her life. Taking the elderly woman off the ventilator had the expected effect, but further debate may have ensued if that had not happened," he says.

"The threshold questions to remove life-prolonging procedures or perhaps more importantly who may make that decision is multistepped. First, the patient must not be capable of making his or her own decisions; and this must be evaluated, determined, and documented by a physician. Check your state laws regarding incapacity. In this case and in Ms. Schiavo's case, there was no question that the patient lacked the capacity to act or decide on their own behalf.

Second, in terms of Florida and many other state laws, prior to the withdrawal of life-prolonging procedures, the incapacitated person must have either a terminal condition, end-stage condition, or be in a persistent vegetative state. Suffering from a debilitating stroke or being in a coma is not necessarily sufficient to meet the second step in the determination, and establishing whether the criteria are met may fall to the courts – particularly when there is doubt as to the patient's wishes," Wolfson continues.

"Critical in the process is determining who can, in the absence of clear and evidenced [preferably written] directives, make those decisions. It appears in the instant case that the spouse was the patient's health surrogate and given that she had a DNR she may have also had a living will and other viable advanced health directive instruments. So residual doubt as to her wishes/intentions would be reduced. Again, this is unlike the circumstance in Ms. Schiavo's case, where the parents and family did not agree with the decisions being made and carried out by Ms. Schiavo's husband, who was her court-appointed guardian. Numerous times over the course of Ms. Schiavo's care and treatment, her parents challenged her husband's guardianship appointment, but it was repeatedly upheld by the courts," he adds.

"We often say that more than anything else, risk management is the exercise of common sense. But we still take a great deal for granted, and sometimes presume that bad case scenarios won't affect us. Consistent, systematized risk management protocols relating to patients who may die in a facility are essential to liability protection. Risk managers should encourage unambiguous means of classifying patients into risk categories. This should serve as a basis for ascertaining if and how patients might be affected by unexpected power outages, changes in temperature – or how staff should respond in the event of a circumstance that could result naturally or otherwise in the patient's death or injury," Wolfson concludes.

Larger Role in Disaster Planning Seen for Quality Managers

When a disaster occurs, otherwise routine health care delivery can be complicated in a number of unexpected ways – and hurricanes Katrina and Rita, it seems, were on a different level than disasters that had occurred in the past. As more than one emergency response expert said, no one will ever again look at disaster planning in quite the same way.

As part of this "new look" at disaster planning, observers say, quality managers should play a larger role in emergency planning and response than they have in the past.

For example, William Cassidy, MD, associate professor of medicine at LSU Health Science Center in Baton Rouge, LA, wishes he had had more quality professionals on his team at the field hospital he oversaw in a former Kmart facility.

A quality manager who knows hospital systems could be invaluable in such a situation, Cassidy observes. "Absolutely, a quality manager could have helped us," he says. "You need someone who is knowledgable but who is also able to scale back to what is effectively a field hospital environment."

Quality managers also can play an important role in disaster response planning, adds Joe Cappiello, BSN, MA, vice president of accreditation field operations for the Joint Commission on Accreditation of Healthcare Organizations (JCAHO).

"Quality managers have a key and important role in sitting at the table to develop response plans," he asserts. "When an organization does a hazard vulnerability assessment, it looks at possible scenarios that may confront that facility – hurricanes if you are in Florida, tornadoes in Kansas, earthquakes in California – or perhaps your town is surrounded by petrochemical plants. We then ask them to sit down and say, is this a situation we might reasonably encounter? All of this should be thought of in the context of how we can give optimal, safe patient care based on the situation with which we are confronted."

If quality managers are to become part of the disaster planning and response team, it is important for them to also learn the lessons of Katrina and Rita and to understand just how different things can be in these situations.

"The first thing they can do is look at the preparation and response to Katrina vs. Rita," says Coppell. "The lessons learned were immediately applied. On the hospital level, I think the lessons that will come out of New Orleans will be very key."

Lessons learned

And what were those lessons? "My own belief is that every one of those accredited hospitals [in New Orleans] had good emergency management plans, conducted drills, and were in compliance," says Cappiello. "With a storm of this size, you had not one but four situations: a hurricane, during which many stood tall and weathered the storm; then the flood; then essentially the loss of all internal support – power, water, sewage; then, a civil disturbance on top of that. A disaster plan must think not only outside of the box but outside of the carton."

Cassidy saw firsthand how difficult things could be. "On Wednesday after the storm, around 7 p.m., they told us we might be putting [a field] hospital in place," he recalls. "Thursday at 4:00, it was confirmed. At 4:30 we did a walk-through of the facility – it lacked lighting, electricity, phone lines, and plumbing. The volunteers from various churches came and started unloading 18-wheelers with supplies, swept and mopped the facility, partitioned up the 'big box' building with plastic Visqueen sheets that we draped on ropes between the pillars to create the 'wards.' At 10:34 p.m. Friday, we were ready to accept patients."

How must a quality manager adapt to such a situation? "First, they cannot be bureaucratic if they are going to get something done that quickly," Cassidy advises. "Also, recognize that normal procedures, like HIPAA, are suspended; credentialing is suspended."

Efficiency is key during disaster response, Cassidy continues. "For example, the only copy of charts would be for people leaving our place to go to someone's home," he explains. "If you go to another hospital or shelter, we would send the chart with you and save a face sheet and maybe a routing sheet. You don't have a copy machine! Our goal is to take stable medical patients and continually flow them out into less acute settings. If you accept your goal as the need to complete medical management of certain patients and move them out, and you have to do it with a skeleton staff, then the redundancy you typically have in a normal hospital has to be suspended."

In addition, the facility did not have infection control at first, Cassidy says. "Volunteers came with food, but instead of putting rolls on single plates, people would just reach in and take the rolls," he notes. "There was no plumbing; we had to rely on people putting antibacterial gel on their hands. So, this was a quality manager's issue: How do you guide people like church volunteers, who are meeting a need but do not have formal training in institutional food presentation?"

Cassidy also cites a specific instance where a quality manager could have offered skills not available from a volunteer. "A quality manager looks into all facets of hospital operations," he notes. "What our volunteer coordinator did was tag along. She told me she saw her role as following along with nurses, doctors, the facility manager, the food person, and hearing that they needed 'X' done and telling the volunteers to get it done. You could see a quality manager tagging along with the other members of the team, and saying, 'OK, you need to have an intake and registration system, a system to move patients between wards, and a way to track their departure. Here's how it's normally done, and here's how the process can be adapted.'"

A unique model?

Having a quality professional intimately involved with disaster planning may not be the norm, but at William Beaumont Hospital in Royal Oak, MI, the chairperson of the emergency management committee is a quality professional – Kay Beauregard, RN, MSA, the facility's director of hospital accreditation and nursing quality, as well as its safety officer.

Beauregard was given this responsibility shortly after 9/11, and to her it makes perfect sense. "It is an interesting overlap," she says, "But there is a relationship. Many quality people oversee patient safety, and this position oversees employee safety. I think more organizations are starting to see this overlap."

"It's a wise place for quality managers to be on the disaster planning committee," says Cappiello. "While we don't by standards mandate who should sit on that, or publish the roster, one would think a common sense approach is you would gather an array of experts who can advise the hospital on the development of plans, assist in the development of drills, and be called upon should disaster strike to provide guidance for the office of emergency management and the administration as they conduct their response."

In her role, Beauregard has overall responsibility for the group that assesses the hospital's risks, what could happen to its infrastructure, events that might possibly occur in the area around them, and what patients they might receive. "Then, based on that information, we put plans in place to try to decrease the likelihood of the events occurring and have a plan in place to respond if they do," she says.

There are other reasons quality managers are well qualified for such responsibility, she continues. "They bring performance improvement expertise, and that's what this is – to take a chaotic situation and organize it into an action plan is similar to taking a quality issue and organizing it into an action plan," she observes.

Many organizations have their emergency departments in charge of this committee, "but we've learned that disasters impact the entire organization, and the rest of the hospital is needed to help the ED to provide resources," Beauregard says. "It involves coordinating bigger issues – like supply chain, electrical outage problems, and so forth – that do not just hinge around the ED."

Quality managers, she continues, also are often involved in regulatory compliance. "Regulators have standards regarding disaster management – they are used to reviewing those standards and making sure the hospital is in compliance."

Beauregard also is among those who believe the disasters will cause everyone involved to take a second look at their own plans. "We are definitely going to review our disaster plan," she says. "This hurricane has taught us that we need to look at issues like sending our hospital staff to respond to disasters outside of ours, whether down the street or in a different state. We need to look at a lot of issues – licensure in other states, liability, workman's comp.

"Internally, we learned we need to revisit our evacuation plan – particularly, how would we evacuate the entire hospital? That's a 'biggy,' because we have over 1,000 beds." ⚐

For more information, contact:

- Kay Beauregard, RN, MSA, Director of Hospital Accreditation and Nursing Quality, William Beaumont Hospital, 3601 W 13 Mile Rd., Royal Oak, MI 48073. Phone: (248) 898-0941. E-mail: kbeauregard@beaumont.edu.

- William Cassidy, MD, Associate Professor of Medicine, LSU Health Science Center, Baton Rouge, LA. E-mail: wcassi@lsuhsc.edu.

- Joe Cappiello, BSN, MA, Vice President, Accreditation Field Operations, Joint Commission on Accreditation of Healthcare Organizations, One Renaissance Blvd., Oakbrook Terrace, IL 60181. Phone: (630) 792-5000.

Health Care Heroes Weather Gulf Storm with Guts and Emergency Planning

Health care workers were heroes of Hurricane Katrina as they worked under grueling conditions to keep their patients alive despite lack of electricity, air conditioning and water, and sewer service.

Surviving the hurricane required more than guts and dedication. How hospitals fared depended on the level of emergency planning put in place before the hurricane hit.

Stories emerged after the hurricane of critically ill patients who died while awaiting evacuation and of doctors and nurses suffering from dehydration and fatigue. But there also were tales of ingenuity, courage, and professionalism amid dire circumstances.

At Tulane University Hospital and Clinic in New Orleans, George Jamison, HCSP, CHCM, GC, director of facility services and safety officer, arrived at work at 7:30 a.m. the Saturday before the storm and began calling in staff and making additional emergency preparations. He didn't leave until the following Friday, on one of the last helicopters to evacuate patients and staff.

Not a single patient at Tulane died during the ordeal, Jamison notes proudly. (Two patients brought to Tulane from nearby Charity Hospital were dead on arrival, he adds.) Visitors, employees, and their family members also fared well.

Before the storm, Jamison and his colleagues had imagined the worst-case scenario – a key component of emergency planning. "You think of every hazard that could happen to you and you prepare for it," says Jamison, who is a surveyor for the Joint Commission on Accreditation of Healthcare Organizations.

Every year, at the beginning of the hurricane season, Jamison stocks a supply of shaving cream, extra clothes, and food. Those are his small steps toward being prepared.

But getting the hospital in shape is a much more daunting task. As Hurricane Katrina approached, it began with a conference call with officials at HCA Corp., the Nashville, TN-based hospital governing body. Jamison conferred with the medical director, the chief nursing officer, the nursing director, the chief of the hospital police, and the head of dietary services.

The hospital called in employees for 1½ times its usual staffing, based on its patient load of about 136. The nurses were staffed for 12-hour shifts; physicians, medical residents, and interns also were called in. At orientation, before they began work at Tulane, they were advised to have emergency plans. Now they had 24 hours to evacuate their families before reporting to work. The hospital was stocked with food and water.

Family members – and their pets – who did not evacuate were placed in the hotel across the street.

Meanwhile, on Saturday, Jamison called in his facilities team: three engineers, a maintenance manager, two electricians, one plumber, three general maintenance workers, a refrigeration specialist, the biomedical equipment director, a technician, and the person who supported the hospital's medical gas supply. He told them all to bring extra clothes and a supply of food.

HCA began stocking supplies at staging areas around the Gulf Coast, with water, food, and linens that could be brought in.

Jamison already had imagined the potential of flooding that submerged the first floor. That flooding would swamp the generator, so he arranged for an additional, 2-megawatt generator to be placed on the mezzanine level. That generator was able to power two elevators, air conditioning, lighting, and medical equipment.

He brought in extra linens and moved the pharmacy, dietary services, and linens from the first floor. He placed huge bags of a kitty litter-type absorbent material on the floors. They were poured into red hazardous waste bags and placed in toilets when the sewage failed, allowing the hospital to maintain hygienic conditions.

Jamison also had about three portable gas generators. Each one was capable of supporting seven ventilators. Jamison wasn't counting on much outside help once the storm hit. "We actually stocked our supplies based on the thought that we wouldn't get that much support from other agencies," he says.

Rescues amid gunfire, chaos

On Monday, after the hurricane passed, but before the levees broke, Tulane received 60 patients and their family members from the Superdome – a total of about 130 people. There were paraplegics, amputees, renal dialysis patients, and elderly people in poor condition. The hospital expected an emergency medical team to accompany them, but they came with no support, and no medical records.

Some family members of hospital employees were able to evacuate Monday afternoon, but by Monday evening, the flood waters had extinguished the hotel's generator. They were plunged into darkness as the city descended into chaos. Gunfire could be heard in the streets outside.

Some family members waded across the street and into the hospital. But Jamison needed to rescue his 79-year-old mother and two dogs. Tuesday evening, Jamison found a rubber rescue boat and, amid the staccato of gunfire, managed to bring his mother and dogs to safety.

Meanwhile, 13 critically ill patients arrived by boat from Charity Hospital. Everyone with nursing credentials – the chief operating officer, the nursing director, the employee health nurse, associate directors of nursing – pitched in to care for patients. When the generator failed from lack of fuel, they worked by flashlight.

Jamison notes the hospital maintained its policies and had a system to "set up command, take control, and communicate." The nurses calmed the patients.

"If you ever want to know what good nurses were made of, it showed there," he says. "It was truly a dedication of the nursing staff, some seasoned nursing and some junior nursing mixed together."

The day before Tulane ran out of fuel, Jamison asked for evacuation plans to begin. "It was actually around noon when I went in and told the COO and CEO and our [HCA] division president, who stayed with us the whole time, that I no longer could support the hospital," he says. "I thought by tomorrow at this time, we wouldn't have fuel. 'I'm telling you that, in my professional opinion, we need to start evacuation procedures immediately.' They contacted HCA corporate, and we started work."

On Thursday, when the elevators failed due to lack of electricity, most patients were already positioned on the second floor, ready for transfer to the garage. Two patients had to be moved by hand – a 350-pound patient and a critically ill heart patient. Both survived the transfer.

Nurses continued to use the portable gas generators for patients on ventilators, but some still had to be manually "bagged" while they awaited evacuation.

Even the evacuation relied on advance planning. Jamison and his colleagues had considered how to turn the top level of the garage into an emergency helicopter landing pad. Bolts on four large lamp standards would need to be sawed off, and the lamps removed, but the garage was capable of holding the weight of the helicopter.

"If we had not done proper preparation, that would not have been possible," he says.

Chapter 3: Coping With Disaster

HCA began arranging privately for helicopters, and flew in body armor for the hospital security force because of the dangerous conditions on the streets. They connected with ham radio operators in Tallahassee, FL, to help guide helicopters in a kind of air traffic control.

"We worked with anybody we could find to get helicopters," says HCA spokesman Ed Fishbough. "We started on it before the storm."

Eventually, HCA found 20 helicopters to use in the evacuation. But with 1,200 people to evacuate, it began slowly. Patients were brought from the swamped Charity hospital to be evacuated from Tulane. The small helicopters could take only one or two patients at a time.

"We found out the airport wasn't being used, [so] we started using it as a triage center," says Fishbough. "[It was an] eight-minute trip to the airport, two minutes on the ground and you're back. The government started to use Louis Armstrong [airport] as a triage center, as well."

The government rescue teams refused to take pets, and Jamison actually contemplated shooting his two boxers rather than abandoning them in the flooded hospital. But HCA offered to take pets as well as people.

"You can't ask people to come in and work and leave their pets behind," says Fishbough. "To them, that's part of their family."

On Thursday night, hospital police said they could not protect all the entrances to the hospital. Patients, employees, and family members moved to the garage, where they spent the night while security officers teamed up to guard the entrances. Everyone was evacuated by Friday afternoon, five days after the storm hit.

After the storm, Jamison moved to Snyder, TX, to stay with his daughter. He immediately began working toward restoring the hospital facility.

Jamison's advice to other hospitals? Follow EC410, the Hazards Vulnerability Analysis standard of the Joint Commission.

"Exercise your plan to the nth degree," he suggests. "Actually call the people [on staff] and say, 'How well prepared are you?' Get [their emergency] names and phone numbers. When you have one of these drills, [think about] what would happen if you had to stay for four days. Could you? Would you?"

Jamison now knows the answer to that question is yes – for himself and his dedicated staff.

Chief Nursing Officer Recounts Katrina Efforts

*[**Editor's note:** This e-mail was written by Pamela McVey, RN, CIC, chief nursing officer at Biloxi (MS) Regional Medical Center, to a chief nursing officer in Natchez, MS. McVey was formerly director of infection control/employee health at the hospital.]*

Well, we just got our e-mail up and running. I hope this actually goes through to you. It must have been your prayers that saved us. If you came down here and saw firsthand the death and destruction on the coast from Ocean Springs to Waveland, MS, you would see that there is NO WAY that Biloxi Regional Medical Center should still be standing!!!

All of our staff, to the best of our knowledge, survived the storm as far as no major injury or death. Everyone is blessed to be alive. However, a large percentage of our staff have suffered catastrophic losses of homes and belongings. Many, many, many of us have lost absolutely everything we own, myself included. My home was in an area, in Pass Christian, that is so badly demolished, that the National Guard and Emergency Operations Center (EOC) cannot even get to it yet. Some of my pets were in a kennel in Pass Christian that more than likely no longer exists. Everyone continues to put all of the personal loss behind them and tend to the patients, our first priority. It is only in the silence of a broken heart, when alone for a few minutes or with a trusted co-worker, that the tears flow briefly. Then it's back to business. I do believe that most of the patients do not know the extent of the loss of the health care workers that are caring for them. And they shouldn't know it. It should not be their burden.

You just would not believe it here. The city of Biloxi has no water, so we have had no water to run our air conditioners. Of course we have had mid 90-degree weather. Inside, it has to be well over 100 degrees. Of course, this also means that we cannot bathe or flush toilets. Think of 100 degrees, nobody bathing, and no toilets flushing. Can you spell "STINK"? We must constantly watch the staff for heat exhaustion in addition to watching the patients for the same thing. We have had only generator power; so needless to say, in order to conserve the generator power, there were frequent and extended times that the elevators were not working. (We have six floors in our hospital.)

We had been cut off from all outside communication. During the storm, we lost cable, so could not monitor the weather. Our EOC radio did not work, the phones went down, and the cell phones would work very sporadically. Windows in patient rooms started flying in and we had to evacuate the patients out of their rooms and into the hallways. As windows continued to fly in and ceiling tiles were ripped from the ceiling, glass was flying all over. We had to try to nail the doors shut, because after a certain time, the broken windows were trying to suck everything out.

We then had to evacuate the sixth-floor patients to the first floor. We no sooner got 38 patients from Med Surg down to the first floor, when it became apparent that the Gulf of Mexico was in our hospital loading dock, just about ready to lap over into the ER.

Things were flying off of our roof, patient rooms were leaking, not really from the roof, but the force of the wind, close to 145 mph, which was driving the rain straight through our bricks. Water was then seeping down onto the ceiling of the floors below and then that started the whole domino effect of ceiling tiles falling, things getting ruined by water coming through the ceiling, etc.

When the storm ended, we were all still alive. We didn't have any idea of what it looked like outside of our little world.

We finally were able to start getting in touch with corporate and once that happened and they started getting a list of our needs, things got mobilized really fast. I can't say enough about [Health Management Associates Inc., owner of the hospital]! They are busting it, trying to get our every need met!

Our sister HMA employees are arriving to help and they are a godsend! Supplies and ice and fuel and clothes and chocolate and our every need is being seen to! You would just bust down and cry if you could see the response from our Mississippi division and all of corporate and our sister hospitals!

Homeland Security is here and there are federal police protecting our ER doors. The National Guard is here, [National Disaster Medical System] is here, and it is overwhelming to see all of this all in and around our beautiful little hospital.

Tonight, for the first time since the storm, we have some air conditioning going. We are not sure how long it will last, but we believe that as we sleep on the floors all over the hospital tonight, we'll get some sleep for the first time. We are running out of food and we do hope that a food truck will reach us tomorrow. It was supposed to have come yesterday and did not make it.

I cannot say enough about the staff of BRMC! Through the entire 12-hour beating, this hospital was, even with moving patients all over to the best area of safety, one step ahead of the storm, and only one of our patients had any anxiety. She was a mom with a potential [pulmonary embolism], with a 4-day-old baby in her arms. That is a tribute to our staff that the patients never panicked because the staff never let on how scared they were. They were calm and confident, professional, and positive.

It has been, and remains, an experience like no other. Yesterday evening, I got my first chance to get out of the building and walk around a little bit. It is 100% totally overwhelming. It smells like death and destruction. It looks like someone dropped a big bomb on us. Almost everything is gone or has been moved to a new location.

Our ER and grounds look like a M.A.S.H. unit. There are injured people everywhere! Our morgue is filling up. There are not enough shelters for the stranded, hungry, thirsty people that are approaching our hospital hourly. We had a young man arrive to our ER and die today with a body temp of 108! We have snakebite victims, people who are already septic with *Vibrio* because of seven-hour swims clinging to trees after having been blown out into the storm.

Our nurses, doctors, techs, therapists, and everyone else has been fantastic throughout! The commitment and dedication to the great responsibility of caring for the patients in our community who have been entrusted to our care and protection has been evident this week. It is an awesome and humbling experience to say that I am their chief nursing officer. With a lesser crew, we would not have survived as long as we have. I can't say that I wish this experience on anyone, but I do know, it is and will continue to be, a life-changing experience. God bless you and thank you for praying for us!

Case Managers Face Challenges Of Hurricane Katrina

For case managers at Our Lady of the Lake Medical Center in Baton Rouge, LA, Hurricane Katrina presented challenges most people can't even imagine.

"As people left New Orleans, Baton Rouge was quickly overwhelmed by the number of patients with special needs. Our Lady of the Lake was the first responder to the special-needs shelter here in Baton Rouge where the majority of people needing medical care were triaged," says Lesley Tilley, RN, BSN, CCM, divisional director of nursing and administrator of medical services.

The hospital's 20 nurse case managers and 13 social workers put in 12-hour days for an entire week, helping keep the situation calm and providing support and care for the patients wherever needed.

The hospital was quickly inundated with hurricane evacuees who had tremendous psycho-social needs, spotty medical records, and no place to go after discharge. Insurance information for most patients was not available, and the web site that approves Medicare days was down.

The patients who came to the hospital had been through a tremendous trauma and needed a sympathetic ear to hear their story.

"During a normal cycle, the case managers go in and assess the patients, develop a plan of care and a discharge plan. They're great at it, but the needs of these patients were overwhelming," Tilley says.

Assessments typically took case managers and social workers twice as long as they would under normal circumstances, and discharge planning was hampered by the fact that there were few places for the patients to go and the transportation services were overwhelmed.

"We would have 20 patients in the hospital ready for discharge, but the staff couldn't just send them home with no place to live. All of these patients needed a place to stay and a ride home," Tilley recalls.

The hospital used its fleet of vans to transport patients back to the special needs shelters and bought bus tickets and airplane tickets for numerous patients whose families were in other areas.

"We didn't want to put them in a shelter if we could avoid it, so we found the family and helped them get home," she says.

The case management department's community resource book was an invaluable resource following Hurricane Katrina. Staff from all parts of the hospital used the information to find community services for their patients.

"Having up-to-date information that is available to everyone in the hospital is a big plus. The case managers and social workers were so overwhelmed that we had to call on the other departments to help with post-acute transfers," Tilley says.

Except for a few patients who were directly admitted from New Orleans hospitals, the majority of patients with health care needs coming out of New Orleans were triaged at two special-needs centers. Baton Rouge hospitals provided the supplies and staff to care for these patients for many days.

Many of the patients who needed hospitalization were directed to Our Lady of the Lake.

"Our hospital is the only one in the area with some special services. We have the largest pediatric unit and pediatric intensive care unit in the city, the only neurosurgical and trauma programs. The doctors tried to triage the patients because they didn't want to overburden our hospital with patients that could be treated elsewhere," she says.

In the first few days following Hurricane Katrina, case managers and social workers at Our Lady of the Lake Medical Center concentrated on crisis management rather than their regular duties, helping the hospital treat and identify community services for the tremendous influx of patients coming from New Orleans.

The social workers spent some of the first few days in the emergency department, helping people who were being discharged find a place to go and assisting them in locating family members so the ED staff could concentrate on treating patients. It was then staffed by the outpatient mental and behavioral health team because the greater need was for the social workers to be on the acute units, Tilley says.

The case managers spent their time at bedsides and in the ED, helping take care of patients. They helped staff a special triage area for patients being transferred from other hospitals.

"When patients came in from other hospitals, the case managers and nurses assessed them, got a physician, and admitted them straight from there," Tilley says.

The hospital set up a prescription writing area, staffed by nurse practitioners and physicians where people who needed only a medication refill could get prescriptions.

Some patients who were transferred to the hospital came with a makeshift medical record. Others came from the special-needs center with just a triage form.

About a dozen patients, mostly infants with heart problems, were transferred to Our Lady of the Lake from Children's Hospital in New Orleans along with their entire record. They were accompanied by nurses and a pediatric heart surgeon.

"Some were airlifted, some came by ambulance, and others were brought in their car by their parents who were desperate to see that their children got care," Tilley says.

Our Lady of the Lake and other Louisiana hospitals go on disaster alert every time there's a hurricane in the Gulf of Mexico, whether it's aimed at Mississippi or Pensacola or Louisiana.

The day before Hurricane Katrina was expected to hit, the disaster plan went into effect. The hospital leaders and department heads made arrangements to stay at the hospital and urged their staff to do so as well.

The hospital set up a child care center in the auditorium for children of employees and accommodated the staff as much as possible.

A command center headed by the administrator on call operated 24 hours a day and coordinated communications with the Louisiana Office of Emergency Preparedness (OEP) and the Louisiana Hospital Association, which coordinated the transfer of patients from other hospitals.

Patient care services set up an employee pool of nonclinical staff to help with the telephones and other duties, freeing up the clinical staff to care for patients.

Every two hours, the hospital called the OEP to let them know how many beds and what kind of beds were available.

Transferring hospitals also called the OEP to see what beds were available for their patients.

The federal law mandating that hospitals have to take any patient that presents was suspended for the first 72 hours following the hurricane, allowing the hospital to send patients with less serious needs to other cities.

"We had all these systems in place for Katrina, but as much as we prepared, the hospital was simply overwhelmed by the influx of patients," Tilley says.

After the arrival of storm evacuees began, case managers in the managed care department e-mailed the payers, notifying them that the case managers were working at the bedside and in the ED taking care of patients and wouldn't be able to conduct utilization reviews in the days following the storm. Nurses from the revenue management department helped during the first week, doing utilization reviews as needed.

A number of patients transferred from New Orleans had insurance from companies that do not contract with Our Lady of the Lake. Those insurers agreed to pay the bill.

More than three weeks after the hurricane hit, the hospital's business office had begun the arduous task of backtracking to determine what kind of insurance coverage the patients they treated had.

The hospital never lost power during the hurricane, although a hospital-owned nursing home two blocks away lost power for two days and many staff members ended up spending the night at the hospital because their homes had no power.

The hospital's capacity is 600, with a normal census in September of 450. Three weeks following the hurricane, the census was 570.

"In the weeks after the hurricane, we rescheduled all the elective surgery that was postponed so we could take care of the patients coming from New Orleans. The hospital is still feeling the effects and trying to catch up," Tilley says. 🏠

For more information, contact:

- Lesley Tilley, RN, BSN, CCM, Divisional Director of Nursing and Administrator of Medical Services, Our Lady of the Lake Medical Center, Baton Rouge, LA. E-mail ltilley@ololrmc.com.

Case Study: Pensacola Hospital and Patients Survive Battering by Hurricane Ivan

It was about 2 a.m., Sept. 16, 2004, when Hurricane Ivan roared into Pensacola, FL, with 130-mile-per-hour winds, battering the boarded-up windows of Sacred Heart Hospital, knocking out the electricity, and forcing the hospital to operate on emergency generators.

Many staff members had arrived at the hospital before the storm hit, anticipating problems with transportation afterward, and they all sprang into action to make sure the patients and more than 2,000 family members of patients and staff being sheltered at the hospital were safe.

"It was pitch black outside, and we heard the awful sound of that wind, but we couldn't see anything," recalls Susan Kearney, LCSW, manager of social services.

Although the windows were boarded up, staff were concerned they might buckle and decided to move the patients from their rooms and into the halls.

Hospital staff were alerted and made their way through the darkened hospital. Within 15 minutes, all 360 patients who were left in the hospital had been moved to the hallways, with oxygen and IV lines still operable.

"The teamwork was amazing. People came from every department and every place in the hospital. Our primary aim was to move the patients and assure them that they were safe and well cared for," she says.

At the same time, the hospital staff became concerned about hundreds of visitors who were sleeping in the lobby, which had large, vulnerable windows. They woke them up and moved them to the basement, where it was quieter and safer.

The next few days called for creativity and patience on the part of the staff and patients, Kearney says.

The hospital regained electricity fairly quickly, but neither the staff's cell phones and pagers nor the hospital's e-mail system worked in the early days after the storm.

"The communication system was really challenged," says Mike Burke, public relations manager for the 449-bed acute care facility, which includes Sacred

Chapter 3: Coping With Disaster

Heart Hospital, Sacred Heart Children's Hospital, and Sacred Heart Women's Hospital.

Managers and leaders from all over the hospital gathered every four hours in a central area to share information about what was happening.

"This is one of the most helpful things we did as a team. This allowed us to be in constant communication with each other, and we could take what we learned back to the staff who were hungry for information in a time of crisis," Kearney says.

Marketing and public relations staff attended the meetings, typed up a summary, and walked through the hospital distributing it to all staff.

The hospital experienced minor damage but no significant structural damage. There was some flooding in the laboratory, caused by water backing up from the air-conditioning unit after the power shut down.

The first few days after the storm, the hospital didn't have water pressure or air conditioning and postponed elective surgery until the following Wednesday, Sept. 22, 2004.

"All of the essential functions of the hospital kept going during the storm. We delivered babies, did heart catheterizations, and emergency surgery," Burke says.

In the two weeks after the storm, the hospital's emergency department visits went up by 40%. Among the injuries were 40 patients injured by chain saws and other serious injuries from falling limbs and falls. The Federal Emergency Management Agency sent a Disaster Medical Assistance Team to the hospital. It set up tents outside the ED to handle minor injuries.

As soon as the storm was over, the social workers and case managers started trying to determine which nursing homes could take patients who were ready for discharge and which patients could be discharged home safely. They made calls to area grocery stores, pharmacies, home health care agencies, and durable medical equipment companies to compile a list of available resources for patients and employees.

They went over the list of patients ready for discharge on a case-by-case basis and thoroughly documented the medical records when the patients couldn't be released because they had no home to go to or no electricity and water. It took as long as 12 days for electricity to be restored to some parts of Pensacola and more than a week before the water was declared safe to drink.

The hospital was waiting to learn whether the extra days would be covered by the patients' insurance. "We wouldn't have done it any differently. These patients couldn't go home and we have plenty of documentation as to why their discharge was delayed," Kearney says.

About a week before Hurricane Ivan struck the Florida panhandle, the hospital started preparing to implement its disaster plan and assigned duties for when the hurricane hit.

The purchasing department stockpiled food, water, medicine, and extra fuel for the hospital's generators, preparing for the possibility of being unable to have supplies delivered for a week.

Four days before the hurricane hit, the hospital began discharging as many patients as it could. Patients who were not ambulatory and who lived in areas that are vulnerable to flooding stayed in the hospital. "When discharges were postponed, we documented as carefully as we could as to the rationale," she says.

The day before the hurricane, the social workers and case managers shifted their attention to the duties they were assigned to handle during the storm. The social work department was assigned to staff the hospital day-care center during the time they were no longer needed for duties on the floor.

The case managers were assigned to the ED to direct people who did not need to be admitted to the hospital to special-needs shelters and other facilities. "We had a lot of frail elderly and people who were on oxygen who came to the hospital because they were afraid. The case manager's role was to direct these patients to appropriate shelters and assist in getting them safely to those shelters," Kearney says.

A shelter in the storm

During the worst of the storm, the hospital provided shelter for more than 2,000 visitors, including children of employees, other family members of employees, and families of patients.

About 20 women in the last stages of pregnancy came into the shelter and slept on recliners provided by the hospital. Several gave birth during the storm.

The hospital provided temporary shelter in its auditorium, the lobbies for the women's hospital and the main hospital, and in the long concourse areas connecting outlying buildings. Many staying in the shelter left the hospital shortly after the storm ended, but some remained for about five days. The day care operated for three weeks.

Kearney's first advice to hospital staff: Accept the fact that a disaster may happen and plan accordingly.

Although the hospital was well prepared for the storm, Kearney contends her department could have been better prepared. She would have stocked up on powerful flashlights, batteries, bottled water, and food for her department.

"Although the hospital fed employees at no cost for two weeks after the storm, we all wished we had planned ahead. We had little flashlights, and trying to make our way around a dark hospital with those little lights was a real challenge," she says. "Prepare as if the disaster is going to hit you head-on," she adds.

Communication is the most vital part of preparation, and hospitals should prepare to operate without their usual communication equipment, she adds.

Make sure your staff have up-to-date information about where the shelters are, what kind of patients they can accommodate, and what kind of patients they can't take, she advises.

Florida Managers Deal with the Effects of Back-to-back Hurricanes

After weathering three major hurricanes in just over 30 days, case managers in Florida hospitals had some advice for their counterparts in other parts of the country: Plan ahead and be flexible.

Here is what some of them experienced:

- Three hospitals in Port Charlotte had to transfer 550 patients to other hospitals because of damage caused by Hurricane Charley.

- Sarasota Memorial Hospital took in 167 special-needs patients and admitted 35 other patients from south Florida hospitals.

- At St. Vincent's Hospital in Jacksonville, as Hurricane Frances approached, the case managers arranged for some patients who lived alone to be discharged to a family member's home or temporarily to an assisted-living center.

When hurricanes Charley, Frances, and Ivan roared into Florida, hospitals in the predicted path of the storms pulled out their disaster plans and prepared to ride out the storms.

Florida hospitals are required by law to have a disaster plan that includes hurricanes and to conduct a disaster plan drill twice a year.

About seven days before a hurricane is expected to hit Florida, the hospitals activate their emergency plan and start making preparations for the possible evacuation and transfer of patients and prepare the physical plant for the storm, says Rich Rasmussen, vice president for strategic communication for the Tallahassee-based Florida Hospital Association.

If the storm appears to be heading toward their area, hospital discharge planners begin the process of identifying patients they can discharge earlier and looking for placements elsewhere in the state for patients who need to stay in the hospital.

The back-to-back storms presented a lot of challenges to discharge planners, says Linda Quick, director of the South Florida Hospital and Healthcare Association.

The hospitals needed to discharge as many patients as possible to free up beds for people who might be injured in the storms, but they often faced challenges in finding safe places for the patients to go.

"It was difficult discharging some of these patients, particularly if they lived alone. The discharge planners had to either find a family member or long-term care unit to take the patients," Quick says.

In fact, a few weeks after Hurricane Charley swept through the southern part of the state, a few elderly or medically fragile patients remained in special-needs shelters because they were on oxygen or a ventilator and still had no power at home.

"It was a very stressful situation for the hospital staff. South Florida hospitals transferred their patients further up north for cardiac catheterization and other interventions, and the patients ended up staying a long time because they had no air conditioning at home," says Mary Ellen Beasley, RN, BSN, division director for case management for HCA's West Florida division, with headquarters in Palm Harbor, FL.

Hospital staff had to copy patient records to send with patients being transferred to other facilities and to make sure the records that went with the patients were accurate, she points out.

Between Hurricane Charley and Hurricane Frances, the case management staff at Sarasota Memorial Hospital began to take a stronger role in coordinating the intake and care of special-needs patients, says Judy Milne, RN, MSN, CHPQ, director of integrated case management and quality improvement.

Because the county does not have a special-needs facility, people from the community who qualified for special-needs care often come to Sarasota Memorial Hospital. During Hurricane Charley, 167 special-needs patients went there.

Under the new plan, the case managers evaluated patients who came to the hospital as Hurricane Frances approached, determining what services, such as oxygen, medication, and home health, they would need when they departed.

"We redesigned the intake process to get more information on the front end to anticipate what we need to do to get these patients back home with the kind of medical support they had prior to the storm," Milne says.

After Hurricane Charley struck, the hospital admitted 35 patients who were evacuated from south Florida hospitals that were closed because of the storm.

"As patients started coming up from south Florida, our hospital filled up quickly. As they recovered, we were in the position of having to transition people to home who didn't have a home. We learned a lot about the whole shelter system," Milne points out.

Shortly after Hurricane Charley hit the state, the hospital sent four case managers to local shelters to help the Red Cross and the state health department find placements for residents who fled their homes in south Florida and who had medical needs. Four case managers worked for two full days coordinating admissions for displaced residents to extended-care facilities and assisted-living facilities.

"We had an increase in people coming to our emergency department. Many were from the hard-hit areas. They couldn't get to their usual physician because the office was blown down and their local hospital wasn't available, so they migrated north," Milne says.

Hurricane Frances presented a different set of challenges, because a large portion of the Sarasota area was left without electricity.

"We had patients who were in the hospital for a few extra days because they had oxygen concentrators that needed electricity or respiratory problems that meant they couldn't handle the humidity with no air conditioning," she says.

Massive evacuation employed

Immediately after the hurricane, 550 patients had to be evacuated to other areas. Hospitals in the Port Charlotte area sustained little damage and had power, but the area's water and sewage system was damaged, making it necessary to evacuate all three hospitals in Charlotte County. The Florida Hospital Association helped facilities transfer the patients, using helicopters provided by Florida hospitals, the Coast Guard, and the National Guard.

"We had to begin shifting those patients north to Tampa, Sarasota, and the Fort Lauderdale area," Rasmussen says. Patients on ventilators had to be evacuated by air by helicopters equipped to handle ventilator patients. Other critically ill patients also were evacuated by air.

Those who did not need immediate assistance were evacuated by ground transportation. "The important thing is that through all three storms, we had thousands of patients transferred across the state without incident. They were safely transported, and their health care continued in a new facility, and we did it all without a single patient's health being compromised," Rasmussen says.

South Florida hospices were challenged, especially if they were in areas where they were having problems providing services. In some cases, families had been dislocated and did not notify the hospice of their location, Quick says.

Chapter 3: Coping With Disaster

Case managers had to use their ingenuity during the storms and power outages, she adds. For instance, some people brought their oxygen with them to the special-needs shelters in their local hospitals, but the oxygen ran out. "They were able to get the company that provides the hospital oxygen to provide some tank oxygen," Quick notes.

When the winds from Hurricane Frances hit Jacksonville, a large number of employees of St. Vincent's Hospital were left with wind-damaged homes and electricity outages.

"We watched the storm carefully and activated our disaster plan. We did a lot of planning at the department level to determine who could get in and who couldn't and to make sure that people came in early if they thought they might not be able to get in for their shift," says Wanda Gibbons, RN, vice president of patient care and chief nursing officer. St. Vincent's is a community hospital licensed for 538 beds, with a 240-bed nursing home on the same campus. The hospital's normal plans for discharge don't always work in the event of a natural disaster, she points out.

"The hurricane made it necessary for our discharge planners to be flexible in working with patients to meet their needs and find a situation where they would be safe," Gibbons adds.

For instance, some patients were discharged to a family member's house instead of their own home or to an assisted-living center for a short time. Just before the storm, staff had some difficulties in placing patients in some area nursing homes that were holding beds in case other facilities had to be evacuated.

As the hurricane approached the area, some staff slept at the hospital to make sure they would be available the next day. Other staff stayed late until the weather lifted. "We didn't want people to be unsafe by driving to work in the middle of the storm," Gibbons says.

Staff who stayed overnight slept in an older nursing unit that used to be a pediatric unit and in the same-day surgery area.

The bridges that cross the St. Johns River, which runs through the middle of Jacksonville, are closed when winds hit 40 miles per hour. "We had to anticipate that the bridges were going to be closed and bring people from the other side of the river in early," she explains.

The hospital arranged for a local cab company to bring in staff who typically ride the bus system or who had other transportation issues.

Chapter 3: Coping With Disaster

In the days before the storm, the discharge planners went into high gear, working to discharge patients who were ready to go home to free up beds in case people were injured in the storm, Gibbons says. "The discharge planners were concerned about not sending someone home who might need to be in a special-needs shelter when the storm hit," she says.

Hospitals throughout the state of Florida staff special-needs shelters for medically fragile, elderly, and disabled people who don't need to be in the hospital but may need medical care or special assistance. For instance, patients on ventilators or those who use oxygen may come into the special-needs shelters because they don't have electricity.

When making plans for rural residents from Florida and south Georgia who come to St. Vincent's for cancer treatment, cardiac, and other specialty care, the discharge planners had to take into account that families who rely on a well for their water could be without a water supply, Gibbons adds.

After paying close attention to three hurricanes with the potential to hit the area, the St. Vincent's staff considered additions to the disaster plan that include an area for family members and a place where staff can bring their pets.

"When school is closed and there's no electricity or telephone service at home, parents are reluctant to leave their children. There is a need for a place for family members to go when we have a disaster," she says.

The hospital also considered setting up an area in a well-ventilated garage where employees could leave their animals in a pet carrier and feed and care for them when they get a break.

"Some people don't know how long it will be before they get home or how long they'll be without electricity. Having their children and pets with them will give them a comfort level they wouldn't have otherwise," Gibbons says.

At Homestead Hospital, as soon as the area was under a hurricane watch, the discharge planners worked aggressively to start early discharge planning, says Jill White, RN, director of case management and performance improvement.

"Once there's a hurricane watch, the community resources start shutting down. The nursing homes stop accepting patients, and home health won't guarantee that they can provide services. It's difficult to place patients during a hurricane watch situation. We have to be very creative," she says. In some cases, patients have come to the hospital emergency department from a nursing home, but the nursing home won't take them back because of the storm. In that case, the hospital provides a safe shelter.

Case management staff pay close attention to the documentation for patients whose length of stay is extended by the storm.

"As long as the insurance companies are open, we work with them trying to set up a plan. They're very aware whether we can get a patient out or not," White explains. Hospital staff concentrate on making sure that patients get the care they need during a disaster and worry about reimbursement later, she says.

"Most of our concern about the payment angle is after the fact. When the storm is headed our way, our top priority is taking care of the patients, making sure they have what they need, and that if they are discharged, it's to a safe place," White says.

Here are some tips from hospital staff who have been through a disaster:

Develop a disaster plan and practice regularly

"You never know what you're going to encounter. Plan for the unthinkable," Rasmussen says, pointing out that Florida was hit with three hurricanes in 30 days with another one looming just afterward.

Plan ahead and know your plans will change as the storm moves through

"The key is to have everything planned out in advance, because during the peak of the storm, you can't do anything except ride it out," notes Gibbons.

For instance, most Florida hospitals have reciprocal arrangements with hospitals in other areas to take their patients in the case of an emergency.

Be flexible and creative

"Sometimes the staff take a lot of encouragement because they're worried about getting here. Our nursing supervisor spent a lot of time telling people how to get here using different routes, and we sent cabs out for people who couldn't come in," Gibbons says.

Constant communication is the key to a successful disaster management plan, Rasmussen says. A few days before the hurricanes hit Florida, the Florida Hospital Association developed a database of key hospital personnel in areas in the path of the storms. The advance planning paid off when Charley hit and disabled Charlotte County emergency operations center, leaving the area with limited communications. The hospital association was able to facilitate communication using its database, he adds.

Plans and Procedures

Chapter Contents

Disaster Preparedness Plan Outline 139

FEMA: 2005 Federal Disaster Declarations 161

Checklist for Infection Control 165

JCAHO Guidance on Emergency Planning 173

Hospital Preparedness Statistics 177

Department and Unit Disaster Sub-plan Templates 179

Disaster Preparedness Plan Outline

*This is from the official web site of Tennessee

I. **Design a "Cover Page" for your plan or use a typed piece of paper. As a minimum it should contain the following information:**

DISASTER PREPAREDNESS PLAN FOR "*Insert the Name of Your Facility,*"

Street address, phone, and fax number. *Date the plan was written*

II. **After the Cover Page insert the following statement:**

This plan complies with the Disaster Preparedness Planning rules set forth by the Tennessee Department of Health, Division of Health Care Facilities; Chapter **1200-8-..-..**, as amended. As a minimum, it is suggested that you include the following information after the above statement: (1) a general statement describing your facility's services to its residents/patients, (2) number of beds or capacity, (3) number of employees, (4) is there only one facility or is your facility part of a corporation, etc.

III. **Emergency Notifications List (A suggested list follows; add to it as needed.)**

MEDICAL, FIRE AND POLICE EMERGENCIES – 911

Fire (Non-Emergency): _____

Emergency Medical Services (EMS) (Non-Emergency): _____

Police Department (Non-Emergency): _____

Sheriff's Department (Non-Emergency): _____

Local Emergency Management Agency
(Business Office): _____

Local Emergency Operations Center (If Activated): _____

Local Electrical Power Provider (Business Office): _____

Local Electrical Power Provider (Emergency Reporting): _____

Local Water Department (Business Office): _____

Local Water Department (Emergency Reporting): _____

Local Telephone Company (Business Office): _____

Local Telephone Company (Emergency Reporting): _____

Local Natural/Propane Gas Supplier (Business Office) _____

Local Natural/Propane Gas Supplier
(Emergency Reporting): _____

Chapter 4: Plans and Procedures

(Review and up-date this list as necessary or **at least once per year**)

IV. **Table of Contents Page should follow the Cover Page.**
A suggested Table Of Contents Page follows:

Purpose	_____ Page 1
Annex A – Fire Safety Procedures	_____ Page ____
Annex B – Tornado/Severe Weather Procedures	_____ Page ____
Annex C – Bomb Threat Procedures (not included)	_____ Page ____
Annex D – Flood Procedures	_____ Page ____
Annex E – Severe Hot and Cold Weather Procedures	_____ Page ____
Annex F – Earthquake Procedures	_____ Page ____
Annex G – Chemical Spills (not included)	_____ Page ____

V. **On the next page write a Purpose Statement or insert the following Purpose**

Statement:

PURPOSE: To continue providing quality care to the residents of "Insert Name of Your Facility" during times of major emergencies and/or disasters or when such events are reasonably believed to be pending by maintaining close coordination and planning links with local emergency response organizations on an ongoing basis.

Chapter 4: Plans and Procedures

GENERAL PREPLANNING NOTES

There are times when a facility must be evacuated for an extended period of time because the structure is unsafe. Depending on the circumstances, there may be one or more similar facilities in your area that are not affected by the same event. Therefore, the following information is provided to assist you in caring for your residents/patients during major emergencies/disasters.

It is recommended that each facility manager meet with the managers of other similar facility managers in his/her area and develop a Memorandum of Understanding/Agreement. The purpose of such an agreement is to form pairings of similar facilities. If your facility must be evacuated, your residents are moved to another similar facility until your facility can be occupied. It is the facility owner's/manager's responsibility to ensure procedures and applicable agreements are in place to move his/her residents/patients to safety.

I have coordinated with Ms. Carol Mace, Division of Health Care Facilities, regarding what constitutes a small facility versus a large facility for emergency preparedness planning purposes. She suggested the following break point: *A small facility is defined as one with one (1) to four (4) employees on any shift. A large facility is defined as one with five (5) or more employees on any shift.*

Large facilities are required to complete the **Staff Functions by Department and Job Assignment** section in each plan Annex. If you own or manage more than one facility and/or you have a corporate office or a staff dedicated to managing more than one facility, you must include these personnel in the Staff Functions by Department and Job Assignment section.

Maps, floor plans, personnel rosters, etc., should be added to the applicable Annex as Appendices. It is important that larger facilities develop an ***alerting or call out*** roster for each Annex. The *Staff Functions by Department and Job Assignment* section of each Annex will aid you in developing an alerting or call out roster.

ANNEX – A

FIRE SAFETY PROCEDURES

1. **MINOR FIRE ACTIONS AND EVACUATION PROCEDURES:** (Division of Health Care Facilities Fire Prevention personnel defined a minor fire as one that is not structural in nature, i.e., fire in a trash can.) It is strongly suggested that you contact the local fire department that would respond to a fire at your facility and work together in determining what size fire, type of fire, and location of fire would constitute a minor fire. Or you might con-

Chapter 4: Plans and Procedures

sider calling the Fire Prevention Specialist(s) at the Division of Health Care Facilities. *A small skillet or sauce pan fire can be extinguished by shutting off the heat source and covering the skillet/pan or by using common table salt.* A dry powder fire extinguisher is also effective but very messy.

- When a fire is detected or smoke from an unknown source is detected, activate pull station fire alarm.
- Begin evacuating all persons from the building.
- If safe to do so, close all interior doors and look for fire location as you evacuate.
- Perform a head count to ensure all persons are out of the building.
- Notify 911 and report your problem for assistance in checking the building for safety purposes.
- Notify the Administrator if he/she is not on property and is not aware of the problem.

2. **STAFF FUNCTIONS BY DEPARTMENT AND JOB ASSIGNMENTS:**
   - Management Personnel
   - Administrative Staff
   - Housekeeping Staff
   - First Aid/Medical Staff
   - Facility Maintenance Staff
   - Food Preparation Staff
   - LIST OTHER Departments and Job Assignments as Applicable

3. **MAJOR FIRE ACTIONS AND EVACUATION PROCEDURES:** A major fire usually involves the structure or a portion of the structure. It could also be a deep fat fryer fire or similar appliance if it is burning out of control. Another major fire source would be (if applicable to your facility) the natural gas line at the side of a facility. If the line is broken, there is always the possibility of ignition. If you facility uses a 500 or 1,000 gallon propane gas tank for heating and/or cooling, there is a potential for leaks, fire, and even an explosion. Once again you are strongly urged to contact the local fire department that would be the first response unit and ask for assistance in determining your facility's potential vulnerability to a major fire.

   - Activate pull station alarm
   - Begin evacuating all persons from the building

- If safe to do so, close all interior doors and look for fire location as you evacuate.
- Perform a head count to ensure all persons are out of the building.
- **<u>Do not re-enter the building.</u>**
- Go to the nearest building that has a phone and ask someone there to call 911.
- Return to the evacuated persons and stay with the evacuees.

4. **FIGHTING THE FIRE:** Fire fighting priorities in order are, *protect human life, protect private property, and protect the environment.* It is suggested that you remove all the residents of your facility to a safe area (evacuate) before attempting to fight a fire. Your local fire department's safety representative is your best source of information and planning assistance. Remember, a MINOR FIRE can become a MAJOR FIRE very quickly.

   - If you reasonably believe the fire to be **<u>minor</u>** in nature and you wish to do so, re-enter the building and use the fire extinguishers.

5. **EVACUATION PROCEDURES:** In your own words describe how your facility will be evacuated, i.e.:

   - Persons in the Recreation Area (TV viewing area) will evacuate the building through the Main Entrance door. If the Main Entrance door is blocked by fire, smoke or other obstacles, evacuate the building through the West Wing Entrance door.
   - Persons in the kitchen area will, if possible, assist in evacuating residents from the Recreation Area. If persons in the kitchen area cannot get to the Recreation Area because of smoke, fire or other obstacles, they will evacuate the building through the Kitchen Entrance door. They should then go around the building to the Main Entrance door and attempt to assist in evacuating the Recreation area.
   - Residents and employees who are in the West Wing when a fire is detected, will evacuate the building by using the West Wing Entrance door.
   - Residents and employees who are in the East Wing when a fire is detected, will evacuate the building by using the East Wing Entrance door.
   - After evacuating the facility, **residents and employees** will assemble on the North side, at least 150 feet from the facility.

   NOTE: *List each area of your facility, including utility room(s) and common area bathrooms and indicate the primary and secondary evacuation routes out of the facility. If your facility is a multi-level (two stories or more; don't forget the basement area) do the same in-depth planning.*

6. **STAFF FUNCTIONS BY DEPARTMENT AND JOB ASSIGNMENTS:**
   - Management Personnel
   - Administrative Staff
   - Housekeeping Staff
   - First Aid/Medical Staff
   - Facility Maintenance Staff
   - Food Preparation Staff
   - LIST OTHER Departments and Job Assignments as Applicable

7. **EXERCISES:** This annex will be exercised at least once per calendar year. Documentation of the annual exercise will include:
   - Date of the exercise: Must be exercised once per year, any time.
   - List the type of fire exercise (MAJOR or MINOR)
   - Results of the exercise: Satisfactory: YES _____ NO _____ (Satisfactory indicates that each Procedure listed above was accomplished safely and in a timely manner.)

A "NO" check mark indicates one or more of the above procedures was not accomplished safely and/or in a timely manner. You should write a very brief description of the problem and the action(s) taken to correct the deficiency. It is recommended that you reaccomplish the portion(s) of the exercise that was unsatisfactory to ensure the revised Procedure(s) will work. A suggested *"Fire Procedures Exercise Record"* sheet follows.

FIRE PROCEDURES Exercise Record

Date of last exercise: _____

Type of exercise: Major fire - _____ Minor fire - _____

Exercise or procedure was satisfactory: YES _____ NO _____

PROCEDURE(S)/POLICIES NEEDING IMPROVEMENT:

1.

2.

3.

4.

Chapter 4: Plans and Procedures

CORRECTIVE ACTION FOR PROCEDURE(S)/POLICIES NEEDING IMPROVEMENT:

1.

2.

3.

4.

5.

ANNEX B

TORNADO/SEVERE WEATHER PROCEDURES

1. When a **SEVERE THUNDERSTORM WATCH** is issued for your area:

   - Notify the Administrator and staff that a Severe Thunderstorm Warning has been issued for your area and include time frame of warning. (Larger facilities may have a designated position to perform this function.)

   - Begin monitoring the storm system on radio, TV or National Oceanographic Atmospheric Administration (NOAA) Weather Alert Radio.

   - Have a battery-powered portable radio available to back up commercial and auxiliary electrical power systems.

2. **STAFF FUNCTIONS BY DEPARTMENT AND JOB ASSIGNMENTS:**

   - Management Personnel
   - Administrative Staff
   - Housekeeping Staff
   - First Aid/Medical Staff
   - Facility Maintenance Staff
   - Food Preparation Staff
   - LIST OTHER Departments and Job Assignments as Applicable

3. When a **SEVERE THUNDERSTORM WARNING** is issued for your area:

   - Notify the Administrator and staff that a Severe Thunderstorm Warning has been issued for your area and include time frame of warning. (Larger facilities may have a designated position to perform this function.)

   - Begin monitoring the storm system on radio, TV or National Oceanographic Atmospheric Administration (NOAA) Weather Alert Radio.

- Have a battery-powered portable radio available to back up commercial and auxiliary electrical power systems.
- Close all exterior doors and windows.
- Keep all persons away from windows.
- Ready pillows and blankets so if weather worsens, you are prepared.
- If any injuries are sustained by Staff members or residents/patients, call 911.
- In case of injury to residents or if residents/patients experience other medical problems, the Administrator will be responsible for ensuring family members of injured or ill residents/patients are notified as soon as possible.
- If there is any damage to the facility and/or surrounding area, call the **Non-Emergency** number *(your Local Emergency Management Director will provide you the department and number to call)*.

NOTE: *Add one or more bullets to the above that states how you will provide emergency food and water for your residents/patients. Your Local Emergency Management Director can provide you with some helpful pre-disaster tips regarding emergency food, water, and other essential supplies.*

4. **STAFF FUNCTIONS BY DEPARTMENT AND JOB ASSIGNMENTS:**
   - Management Personnel
   - Administrative Staff
   - Housekeeping Staff
   - First Aid/Medical Staff
   - Facility Maintenance Staff
   - Food Preparation Staff
   - LIST OTHER Departments and Job Assignments as Applicable

5. **TORNADO WATCH:**
   - Notify the Administrator and staff that a Tornado Watch has been issued for your area and include time frame of warning.
   - Begin monitoring the storm system on radio, TV or National Oceanographic Atmospheric Administration (NOAA) Weather Alert Radio.
   - Have a battery-powered portable radio available to back up commercial and auxiliary electrical power systems.

- Be prepared to transition from a Tornado Watch to a Tornado Warning with little or no advance warning.

6. **STAFF FUNCTIONS BY DEPARTMENT AND JOB ASSIGNMENTS:**
   - Management Personnel
   - Administrative Staff
   - Housekeeping Staff
   - First Aid/Medical Staff
   - Facility Maintenance Staff
   - Food Preparation Staff
   - LIST OTHER Departments and Job Assignments as Applicable

7. **TORNADO WARNING:**
   - Notify the Administrator and staff that a Tornado Warning has been issued for your area and include time frame of warning.
   - Close all exterior doors and windows.
   - Close all interior doors.
   - Ensure all Staff members and residents are moved to the interior hallways and have a pillow and blanket.

   NOTE: *If your facility has a basement, move everyone to the basement instead of hallways. Staff members and residents will remain at their Tornado Warning shelter area until the warning has expired and/or the storm cloud has passed.*

8. **STAFF FUNCTIONS BY DEPARTMENT AND JOB ASSIGNMENTS:**
   - Management Personnel
   - Administrative Staff
   - Housekeeping Staff
   - First Aid/Medical Staff
   - Facility Maintenance Staff
   - Food Preparation Staff
   - LIST OTHER Departments and Job Assignments as Applicable

9. **AFTER THE TORNADO/WINDS HAVE PASSED:**
   - Check Staff members and residents/patients for injuries.

- If there are injuries, call 911, if the telephone is operable. You may have to try and use a cellular phone, neighbor's phone, nearby business phone or pay phone.

NOTE: *Cellular phone systems are usually useless immediately after an event occurs because everyone, including first responders, overload the system.*

- Check the facility and immediate outside area for damages.

    A. Electricity – Does the facility have electrical power? Look for downed power lines, trees on lines and/or storm debris on power lines.

    B. Water – Does water flow when faucets are turned ON? Is the water color normal? Does it have an unusual odor?

    C. Gas (if applicable) – Do gas appliances work when turned ON? Is a there an odor of gas (rotten eggs)? Are gas lines/regulators outside the facility intact?

NOTE: *If your facility has a residential propane storage tank, is it still upright? Is the fuel supply line from the tank to your facility intact? If you suspect a leak or hear a high pressure, hissing or whistling sound, release in progress, move everyone upwind and uphill from the leak and extinguish or guard against potential ignition sources.*

    D. Look at damage to the facility and use your judgement as to whether or not it is safe to occupy the facility. If you determine the building is unsafe for occupancy, notify the Local Emergency Management Agency by calling

    _____.

    E. If an evacuation of "Insert Name of Your Facility" is necessary, residents/patients and Staff members will move to "Insert the Name, Street Address, Phone Number, and Name of the Receiving Facility."

NOTE: *Your Local Emergency Management Director will provide you with the number to call. It is recommended that you use the* **Pairing Principle** *discussed at the NOTE shown on the page before Annex A. Prior to moving your residents, you should coordinate the evacuation with the Local Emergency Management Agency to ensure the roads/streets between your facility and the receiving facility are passable.*

    F. Look for anything else that might be of Disaster Intelligence value to the local response officials and report the information.

Chapter 4: Plans and Procedures

- The Administrator will ensure family members of the residents/patients are notified as soon as possible concerning any medical problems, injuries and/or evacuation of the facility.

9. **STAFF FUNCTIONS BY DEPARTMENT AND JOB ASSIGNMENTS:**
   - Management Personnel
   - Administrative Staff
   - Housekeeping Staff
   - First Aid/Medical Staff
   - Facility Maintenance Staff
   - Food Preparation Staff
   - LIST OTHER Departments and Job Assignments as Applicable

10. **EXERCISES**: This annex will be exercised at least once per calendar year.

    Documentation of the annual exercise will include:
    - Date of the exercise: Must be accomplished prior to **MARCH** each year.
    - List the type of severe weather exercise (THUNDERSTORM or TORNADO):
    - Results of the exercise: Satisfactory: YES ____ NO ____ (Satisfactory indicates that each Procedure listed above was accomplished safely and in a timely manner.)

    A "NO" check mark indicates one or more of the above procedures was not accomplished safely and/or in a timely manner. You should write a very brief description of the problem and the action(s) taken to correct the deficiency. It is recommended that you reaccomplish the portion(s) of the exercise that was unsatisfactory to ensure the revised Procedure(s) will work. A suggested "Tornado/Severe Weather Procedures Exercise Record" sheet follows.

TORNADO/SEVERE WEATHER Exercise Record

Date of last exercise: _____

Type of exercise: THUNDERSTORM - ____ TORNADO - ____

Exercise of procedures was *satisfactory*: YES ___ NO ___

PROCEDURE(S)/POLICIES NEEDING IMPROVEMENT:

   1.

Disaster Preparedness for Healthcare Facilities

2.

3.

4.

CORRECTIVE ACTION FOR PROCEDURE(S)/POLICIES NEEDING IMPROVEMENT:

1.

2.

3.

4.

5.

ANNEX D

FLOODING

1. **FLOOD PLAIN STATUS:** (Select the appropriate statement shown below. If you are unsure about being in or out of a flood plain, ask you Local Emergency Management Office.)

    - "Insert the Name of Your Facility" is not located in a flood plain.
    - "Insert the Name of Your Facility" is located in a flood plain.

2. FLOOD WATCH: Flooding is possible.

    - Monitor National Oceanographic and Atmospheric Administration (NOAA) radio or commercial radio or TV for additional information.
    - Be prepared to evacuate to higher ground.

3. **STAFF FUNCTIONS BY DEPARTMENT AND JOB ASSIGNMENTS:**

    - Management Personnel
    - Administrative Staff
    - Housekeeping Staff
    - First Aid/Medical Staff
    - Facility Maintenance Staff
    - Food Preparation Staff
    - LIST OTHER Departments and Job Assignments as Applicable

Chapter 4: Plans and Procedures

4. **FLOOD WARNING**: Flooding is occurring in your area or will occur soon.
   - Prepare to evacuate your facility.
   - Monitor National Oceanographic and Atmospheric Administration (NOAA) radio or commercial radio or TV.
   - If you are paired with a facility outside the projected flood waters, you may want to evacuate before being asked to evacuate by the authorities.
   - If you decide to evacuate your facility and go to higher ground, call and coordinate your evacuation with the Local Emergency Management Office. The roads you want to travel may already be underwater. (The Local Emergency Management Director will provide you with the number to call.)

5. **STAFF FUNCTIONS BY DEPARTMENT AND JOB ASSIGNMENTS:**
   - Management Personnel
   - Administrative Staff
   - Housekeeping Staff
   - First Aid/Medical Staff
   - Facility Maintenance Staff
   - Food Preparation Staff
   - LIST OTHER Departments and Job Assignments as Applicable

6. **FLASH FLOOD WATCH**: Flash Flooding is possible. A flash flood can occur without warning.

7. **STAFF FUNCTIONS BY DEPARTMENT AND JOB ASSIGNMENTS:**
   - Management Personnel
   - Administrative Staff
   - Housekeeping Staff
   - First Aid/Medical Staff
   - Facility Maintenance Staff
   - Food Preparation Staff
   - LIST OTHER Departments and Job Assignments as Applicable

NOTE: *If your facility is in an area that has a history of flash flooding, it is strongly suggested that you use this part of the Annex to list those minimum things your staff should do when a flash flood watch is issued.*

Disaster Preparedness for Healthcare Facilities

Chapter 4: Plans and Procedures

8. **FLASH FLOOD WARNING:** A Flash Flood is occurring.

9. **STAFF FUNCTIONS BY DEPARTMENT AND JOB ASSIGNMENTS:**
   - Management Personnel
   - Administrative Staff
   - Housekeeping Staff
   - First Aid/Medical Staff
   - Facility Maintenance Staff
   - Food Preparation Staff
   - LIST OTHER Departments and Job Assignments as Applicable

   NOTE: *If your facility is in a flash flood-prone area, it is recommended that you use the facility pairing principle in your pre-planning process.*

10. **EVACUATION:**
    - Notify the administrator.
    - Call the Local Emergency Management Agency at _____ and let them know you are evacuating your facility. (The Local Emergency Management Office will provide you with the number to call.)
    - Ensure residents/patients carry prescription medications with them.
    - The administrator will ensure families of employees and residents patients are notified as necessary.

11. **STAFF FUNCTIONS BY DEPARTMENT AND JOB ASSIGNMENTS:**
    - Management Personnel
    - Administrative Staff
    - Housekeeping Staff
    - First Aid/Medical Staff
    - Facility Maintenance Staff
    - Food Preparation Staff
    - LIST OTHER Departments and Job Assignments as Applicable

12. **AFTER THE FLOOD:**
    - Do not turn on or plug in any electrical appliances until told to do so by a qualified electrician.
    - Do not turn on gas appliances until told to do so by a qualified gas system technician.

- Prepare an inventory of loses associated with flooding of the facility.
- Take photographs and/or video footage of the facility.
- Report any damages and approximate dollar value to your Local Emergency Management Agency.

13. **STAFF FUNCTIONS BY DEPARTMENT AND JOB ASSIGNMENTS:**
    - Management Personnel
    - Administrative Staff
    - Housekeeping Staff
    - First Aid/Medical Staff
    - Facility Maintenance Staff
    - Food Preparation Staff
    - LIST OTHER Departments and Job Assignments as Applicable

14. **EXERCISES:** This annex will be exercised at least once per calendar year.

    Documentation of the annual exercise will include:
    - Date of the exercise: FLOODING exercise must be accomplished prior to *MARCH* each year.
    - List the type of flooding exercise (FLOOD or FLASH FLOOD):
    - Results of the exercise: Satisfactory: YES _____ NO _____ (Satisfactory indicates that each Procedure listed above was accomplished safely and in a timely manner.)

    A "NO" check mark indicates one or more of the above procedures was not accomplished safely and/or in a timely manner. You should write a very brief description of the problem and the action(s) taken to correct the deficiency. It is recommended that you reaccomplish the portion(s) of the exercise that was unsatisfactory to ensure the revised Procedure(s) will work. A suggested "Flooding Procedures Exercise Record" sheet

FLOODING Exercise Record

Date of last exercise: _____

Type of exercise: FLOOD - _____ FLASH FLOOD - _____

Exercise of procedures was *satisfactory*: YES ___ NO ___

PROCEDURE(S)/POLICIES NEEDING IMPROVEMENT:

1.

2.

3.

4.

CORRECTIVE ACTION FOR PROCEDURE(S)/POLICIES NEEDING IMPROVEMENT:

1.

2.

3.

4.

ANNEX E

SEVERE HOT AND COLD WEATHER PROCEDURES

1. COLD WEATHER:

NOTE: *Under normal circumstances the facility's heating unit(s) will provide a comfortable environment. The following steps should be taken when/if the facility's heating unit(s) become inoperative.*

- Notify the appropriate heating repair personnel.
- If the heating repair company indicates an unusual amount of time to repair the unit, consider relocating to a paired facility.
- If you decide to move to another facility, notify your Local Emergency Management Office for coordination purposes.
- If an evacuation of the facility is necessary, the Administrator will ensure family members are notified.
- Keep persons dressed warmly.
- Get blankets ready for use in case they are needed.
- Provide warm liquids for residents.
- If feasible for your facility and if it can be done safely, consider using portable gas heaters.

- If electrical power is interrupted for more than five (5) minutes, notify theAdministrator.

NOTE: *Indicate how you intend to provide and prepare food for your residents.*

2. **STAFF FUNCTIONS BY DEPARTMENT AND JOB ASSIGNMENTS:**
   - Management Personnel
   - Administrative Staff
   - Housekeeping Staff
   - First Aid/Medical Staff
   - Facility Maintenance Staff
   - Food Preparation Staff
   - LIST OTHER Departments and Job Assignments as Applicable

3. **HOT WEATHER:**

NOTE: *Under normal circumstances the facility's cooling unit(s) will provide a comfortable environment. The following steps should be taken when/if the facility's cooling unit(s) become inoperative.*

- Notify the appropriate air conditioning repair personnel.
- If the air conditioning repair company indicates an unusual amount of time to repair the unit, consider relocating to a paired facility.
- If you decide to move to another facility, notify your Local Emergency Management Office for coordination purposes.
- If an evacuation of the facility is necessary, the Administrator will ensure family members are notified.
- If a person appears to be in any danger of heat-related stress, call 911.
- Provide cool liquids for persons to drink.
- Use fans to circulate air.
- Provide cold wash cloths as needed.
- If electrical power is interrupted for more than five minutes, notify the Administrator.

NOTE: *Indicate how you intend to provide and prepare food for your residents.*

4. **STAFF FUNCTIONS BY DEPARTMENT AND JOB ASSIGNMENTS:**
   - Management Personnel
   - Administrative Staff
   - Housekeeping Staff
   - First Aid/Medical Staff
   - Facility Maintenance Staff
   - Food Preparation Staff
   - LIST OTHER Departments and Job Assignments as Applicable

5. **EXERCISES:** This annex will be exercised at least once per calendar year. Documentation of the annual exercise will include:
   - Date of the exercise: Severe Weather HOT exercise must be accomplished prior to **MAY** each year. COLD Weather exercise must be accomplished prior to **NOVEMBER** each year.
   - List the type of severe weather hot/cold exercise (HOT or COLD):
   - Results of the exercise: Satisfactory: YES _____ NO _____ (Satisfactory indicates that each Procedure listed above was accomplished safely and in a timely manner.)

   A "NO" check mark indicates one or more of the above procedures was not accomplished safely and/or in a timely manner. You should write a very brief description of the problem and the action(s) taken to correct the deficiency. It is recommended that you reaccomplish the portion(s) of the exercise that was unsatisfactory to ensure the revised Procedure(s) will work. A suggested "Severe Weather Hot/Cold Procedures Exercise Record" sheet follows.

SEVERE WEATHER HOT/COLD Exercise Record

Date of last exercise: _____

Type of severe weather HOT/COLD Exercise: HOT ___ COLD ___

Exercise of procedures was *satisfactory*: YES ___ NO ___

PROCEDURE(S)/POLICIES NEEDING IMPROVEMENT:

1.

2.

Chapter 4: Plans and Procedures

    3.

    4.

CORRECTIVE ACTION FOR PROCEDURE(S)/POLICIES NEEDING IMPROVEMENT:

    1.

    2.

    3.

    4.

ANNEX E

EARTHQUAKE PROCEDURES

NOTE: *You will have no warning before an earthquake occurs.*

1. **DURING THE EARTHQUAKE:**

   - When the shaking begins, get under the nearest piece of heavy furniture, wedge yourself in a doorway, get under a bed or in a bathtub and hold on.
   - Do not attempt to go outside until the shaking has stopped.
   - Most earthquake-related injuries occur from falling objects.

   NOTE: *It is not recommended to attempt to take any action (job assignments) while an earthquake is occurring except TAKE COVER and hang on.*

2. **AFTER THE SHAKING STOPS:**

   - Check yourself and those near your for injuries.
   - Perform simple rescues such as removing victims from under lightweight debris.
   - To the best of your ability, assess the number and types of injuries at your facility.
   - If the facility appears to be structurally unsafe, evacuate to an open outside An area that is free of trees, overhead power lines, adjacent tall structures, etc. An aftershock can occur at any time and cause previously damaged buildings to collapse.
   - Telephones may or may not work. If you have a working phone, DO NOT use it unless you have a medical, fire or Hazardous Materials emergency.

Using your phone may cause the system to fail.

- Turn off all utilities and leave them off until you are told it is safe to turn them on.
- All off-duty personnel should automatically report for duty if they can reach the facility safely. They should ensure their family members are safe before reporting.
- Do not use the phone to call in off-duty personnel.

3. **STAFF FUNCTIONS BY DEPARTMENT AND JOB ASSIGNMENTS**:
   - Management Personnel
   - Administrative Staff
   - Housekeeping Staff
   - First Aid/Medical Staff
   - Facility Maintenance Staff
     - Food Preparation Staff
     - LIST OTHER Departments and Job Assignments as Applicable

4. **EXERCISES**: This annex will be exercised at least once per calendar year.

   Documentation of the annual exercise will include:
   - Date of the exercise: (Must be exercised once per year, any time.)
   - List the type of exercise: EARTHQUAKE
   - Results of the exercise: Satisfactory: YES _____ NO _____ (Satisfactory indicates that each Procedure listed above was accomplished safely and in a timely manner.)

   A "NO" check mark indicates one or more of the above procedures was not accomplished safely and/or in a timely manner. You should write a very brief description of the problem and the action(s) taken to correct the deficiency. It is recommended that you reaccomplish the portion(s) of the exercise that was unsatisfactory to ensure the revised Procedure(s) will work. A suggested "Earthquake Procedures Exercise Record" sheet follows.

EARTHQUAKE Exercise Record

Date of last exercise: _____

Type of exercise: EARTHQUAKE

Exercise of procedures was *satisfactory*: YES ___ NO ___

PROCEDURE(S)/POLICIES NEEDING IMPROVEMENT:

1.

2.

3.

4.

CORRECTIVE ACTION FOR PROCEDURE(S)/POLICIES NEEDING IMPROVEMENT:

1.

2.

3.

4.

Source: The Official Web Site of Tennessee http://www.tnema.org/Library/Medical/HLTHPLAN.PDF

FEMA: 2005 Federal Disaster Declarations

MAJOR DISASTER DECLARATIONS

Number	Date	State	Title
1620	12/20	South Dakota	Severe Winter Storm
1619	12/16	Connecticut	Severe Storms and Flooding
1618	12/09	Alaska	Severe Fall Storm, Tidal Surges, and Flooding
1617	12/01	Kentucky	Severe Storms and Tornadoes
1616	11/21	North Dakota	Severe Winter Storm and Record and/or Near Record Snow
1615	11/15	Kansas	Severe Storms and Flooding
1614	11/10	Massachusetts	Severe Storms and Flooding
1613	11/10	Puerto Rico	Severe Storms, Flooding, Landslides, and Mudslides
1612	11/08	Indiana	Tornado and Severe Storms
1611	11/09	Northern Mariana Islands	Typhoon Nabi
1610	10/26	New Hampshire	Severe Storms and Flooding
1609	10/24	Florida	Hurricane Wilma
1608	10/07	North Carolina	Hurricane Ophelia
1607	09/24	Louisiana	Hurricane Rita
1606	09/24	Texas	Hurricane Rita
1605	08/29	Alabama	Hurricane Katrina
1604	08/29	Mississippi	Hurricane Katrina
1603	08/29	Louisiana	Hurricane Katrina
1602	08/28	Florida	Hurricane Katrina
1601	08/23	Louisiana	Tropical Storm Cindy
1600	08/23	Kansas	Severe Storms and Flooding
1599	08/22	Wyoming	Tornado
1598	08/01	Utah	Flood and Landslide
1597	07/22	North Dakota	Severe Storms, Flooding, and Ground Saturation
1596	07/22	South Dakota	Severe Storm
1595	07/10	Florida	Hurricane Dennis
1594	07/10	Mississippi	Hurricane Dennis
1593	07/10	Alabama	Hurricane Dennis
1592	07/06	Idaho	Heavy Rains and Flooding
1591	06/29	Maine	Severe Storms, Flooding, Snow Melts, and Ice Jams
1590	06/23	Nebraska	Severe Storms and Flooding
1589	04/19	New York	Severe Storms and Flooding
1588	04/19	New Jersey	Severe Storms and Flooding
1587	04/14	Pennsylvania	Severe Storms and Flooding
1586	04/14	Arizona	Severe Storms and Flooding
1585	04/14	California	Severe Storms, Flooding, Landslides, and Mud and Debris Flows
1584	03/14	Alaska	Severe Winter Storm
1583	03/07	Nevada	Heavy Rains and Flooding

MAJOR DISASTER DECLARATIONS (continued)

1582	02/18	American Samoa	Tropical Cyclone Olaf, including High Winds, High Surf, and Heavy Rainfall
1581	02/17	Arizona	Severe Storms and Flooding
1580	02/15	Ohio	Severe Winter Storms, Flooding and Mudslides
1579	02/08	Kansas	Severe Winter Storms, Heavy Rains, and Flooding
1578	02/08	Kentucky	Severe Winter Storm and Record Snow
1577	02/04	California	Severe Storms, Flooding, Debris Flows, and Mudslides
1576	02/01	Utah	Severe Storms and Flooding
1575	02/01	Hawaii	Severe Storms and Flash Flooding
1574	02/01	West Virginia	Severe Storms, Flooding, and Landslides
1573	01/21	Indiana	Severe Winter Storms and Flooding

EMERGENCY DECLARATIONS

Number	Date	State	Title
3264	10/19	Massachusetts	Severe Storms and Flooding
3263	09/30	Delaware	Hurricane Katrina Evacuation
3262	09/30	New York	Hurricane Katrina Evacuation
3261	09/21	Texas	Hurricane Rita
3260	09/21	Louisiana	Hurricane Rita
3259	09/20	Florida	Tropical Storm Rita
3258	09/19	New Hampshire	Hurricane Katrina Evacuation
3257	09/19	New Jersey	Hurricane Katrina Evacuation
3256	09/19	Maine	Hurricane Katrina Evacuation
3255	09/19	Rhode Island	Hurricane Katrina Evacuation
3254	09/14	North Carolina	Hurricane Ophelia
3253	09/13	Montana	Hurricane Katrina Evacuation
3252	09/13	Massachusetts	Hurricane Katrina Evacuation
3251	09/13	Maryland	Hurricane Katrina Evacuation
3250	09/13	Ohio	Hurricane Katrina Evacuation
3249	09/13	Wisconsin	Hurricane Katrina Evacuation
3248	09/13	California	Hurricane Katrina Evacuation
3247	09/13	North Dakota	Hurricane Katrina Evacuation
3246	09/13	Connecticut	Hurricane Katrina Evacuation
3245	09/13	Nebraska	Hurricane Katrina Evacuation
3244	09/13	Idaho	Hurricane Katrina Evacuation
3243	09/13	Nevada	Hurricane Katrina Evacuation
3242	09/13	Minnesota	Hurricane Katrina Evacuation
3241	09/12	Arizona	Hurricane Katrina Evacuation
3240	09/12	Virginia	Hurricane Katrina Evacuation
3239	09/10	Iowa	Hurricane Katrina Evacuation
3238	09/10	Indiana	Hurricane Katrina Evacuation

EMERGENCY DECLARATIONS (continued)

3237	09/10	Alabama	Hurricane Katrina Evacuation
3236	09/10	Kansas	Hurricane Katrina Evacuation
3235	09/10	Pennsylvania	Hurricane Katrina Evacuation
3234	09/10	South Dakota	Hurricane Katrina Evacuation
3233	09/10	South Carolina	Hurricane Katrina Evacuation
3232	09/10	Missouri	Hurricane Katrina Evacuation
3231	09/10	Kentucky	Hurricane Katrina Evacuation
3230	09/07	Illinois	Hurricane Katrina Evacuation
3229	09/07	New Mexico	Hurricane Katrina Evacuation
3228	09/07	Oregon	Hurricane Katrina Evacuation
3227	09/07	Washington	Hurricane Katrina Evacuation
3226	09/07	District of Columbia	Hurricane Katrina Evacuation
3225	09/07	Michigan	Hurricane Katrina Evacuation
3224	09/05	Colorado	Hurricane Katrina Evacuation
3223	09/05	Utah	Hurricane Katrina Evacuation
3222	09/05	North Carolina	Hurricane Katrina Evacuation
3221	09/05	West Virginia	Hurricane Katrina Evacuation
3220	09/05	Florida	Hurricane Katrina Evacuation
3219	09/05	Oklahoma	Hurricane Katrina Evacuation
3218	09/05	Georgia	Hurricane Katrina Evacuation
3217	09/05	Tennessee	Hurricane Katrina Evacuation
3216	09/02	Texas	Hurricane Katrina
3215	09/02	Arkansas	Hurricane Katrina
3214	08/28	Alabama	Hurricane Katrina
3213	08/28	Mississippi	Hurricane Katrina
3212	08/27	Louisiana	Hurricane Katrina
3211	04/28	New Hampshire	Snow
3210	04/21	Maine	Snow
3209	04/01	Maine	Snow
3208	03/30	New Hampshire	Snow
3207	03/30	New Hampshire	Snow
3206	03/14	Maine	Snow
3205	03/14	Maine	Snow
3204	02/23	Nevada	Snow
3203	02/17	Rhode Island	Snow
3202	02/17	Nevada	Snow
3201	02/17	Massachusetts	Snow
3200	02/17	Connecticut	Snow
3199	02/01	Illinois	Snow
3198	01/11	Ohio	Snow
3197	01/11	Indiana	Snow

FIRE MANAGEMENT ASSISTANCE DECLARATIONS

Number	Date	State	Incident
2595	12/29	Oklahoma	Eastern Oklahoma County Fire Complex
2594	12/28	Oklahoma	Achille Fire Complex
2593	12/28	Texas Kennedale	Fire
2592	12/28	Oklahoma	Hughes County Fire Complex
2591	12/28	Texas	Callahan County Fire
2590	12/02	Oklahoma	Texanna Road Fire
2589	11/30	Oklahoma	Antioch Fire
2588	11/30	Oklahoma	Velma Complex Fire
2587	11/29	Oklahoma	Flat Rock Complex Fire
2586	11/18	California	School Fire
2585	10/06	California	Border 50 Fire
2584	10/06	California	Woodhouse Fire
2583	09/28	California	Topanga Fire
2582	09/05	California	Sundevil Fire
2581	08/29	Nevada	Chance Fire
2580	08/26	California	Manton Fire
2579	08/25	Oregon	Deer Creek
2578	08/22	Nevada	Vor-McCarty Fire
2577	08/19	Hawaii	Waikele Fire
2576	08/15	Hawaii	Nanakuli Brush Fire
2575	08/07	Washington	School Fire
2574	08/04	Hawaii	Akoni Pule Highway Fire
2573	08/02	Hawaii	Lalamilo Fire
2572	08/01	Washington	Dirty Face Fire
2571	07/25	California	Quartz Fire
2570	07/22	Arizona	Edge Fire Complex
2569	07/16	South Dakota	Skyline #2 Fire
2568	07/16	Nevada	Carlin Fire
2567	07/16	Nevada	Contact Fire
2566	07/10	Colorado	Mason Fire
2565	07/10	South Dakota	Ricco Fire
2564	06/27	Utah	Blue Springs Fire
2563	06/24	Nevada	Good Springs Fire
2562	06/23	Arizona	Humbug Fire
2561	06/22	Arizona	Cave Creek Fire Complex
2560	06/12	Arizona	Hulet Fire
2559	06/08	Arizona	Bobby Fire
2558	05/26	Arizona	Vekol Fire
2557	04/19	South Dakota	Camp Five Fire

Checklist for Infection Control

Concerns when reopening healthcare facilities closed due to extensive water and wind damage

Prior to opening a health care facility that has undergone extensive water and wind damage, inspections need to be conducted to determine if the building is salvageable. If the decision is made to proceed with recovery and remediation, building and life safety inspections must be completed before any restoration work is done to the facility. Parts I-IV describe those activities that need to be completed. Parts V-VII provide guidance for infection control review of facilities to be done before the hospital can reopen.

Prior to opening any portion of a facility such as emergency rooms or clinics, adequate support services need to be available to provide quality care in a safe environment. Contracting with outside services could be considered.

Certification for occupancy must be obtained prior to reopening the facility. Regulations regarding health care facility certification and licensing differ from state to state. Refer to specific state and local government resources for more information.

I. Safety Evaluation

   The following should be evaluated by facilities experts:
   - structural integrity and missing structural items
   - assessment of hidden moisture
   - electrical system damage, including high voltage, insulation, and power integrity
   - water distribution system damage
   - sewer system damage
   - fire emergency systems damage
   - air handling system damage
   - medical waste and sharps disposal system

II. Water Removal

   Water should be removed as soon as possible once the safety of the structure has been verified.
   - pump out standing water

- wet vacuum residual wetness from floors, carpets, and hard surfaces
- clean wet vacuums after use and allow to dry

III. Water Damage Assessment and Mold Remediation

- open the windows in the damaged areas of the building during remediation
- remove porous items that have been submerged or have visible mold growth or damage
- minimize dispersion of mold spores by covering the removed items and materials with plastic sheeting (dust-tight chutes leading to dumpsters outside the building may be helpful)
- dispose these items as construction waste
- seal off the ventilation ducts to and from the remediation area and isolate the work area from occupied spaces, if the building is partially occupied
- scrub and clean hard surfaces with detergents to remove evident mold growth (If a biocide is used, follow manufacturer's instructions for use and ventilate the area. Do not mix chlorine-containing biocides with detergents or biocides containing ammonia.)
- dry the area and remaining items and surfaces
- evaluate the success of drying and look for residual moisture in structural materials (Moisture-detection devices [e.g., moisture meters] or borescopes could be used in this evaluation.)
- remove and replace structural materials if they cannot be dried out within 48 hours

IV. Inspect, Repair, Disinfect where Appropriate, or Replace Facility Infrastructure

- HVAC system (motors, duct work, filters, insulation) inspection, disinfection, repair and replacement
- water system (cold and hot water, sewer drainage, steam delivery, chillers, boilers)
- steam sources (if piped in from other places, e.g., utility companies, it will impact autoclaves)
- electrical system (wiring, lighting, paging and patient call systems, emergency generators, fire alarms)
- electronic communication systems (telephones, paging and patient call systems, computers)

- medical gas system
- hazardous chemicals/radioactive storage

V. General Inventory of Areas with Water and Wind Damage

- What furniture can be salvaged? discard wet porous furniture that cannot be dried and disinfected (including particle board furniture) disinfect furniture with non-porous surfaces and salvage discard upholstered furniture, drapery, and mattresses if they have been under water or have mold growth or odor discard all items with questionable integrity or mold damage

- What supplies can be salvaged? salvage linens and curtains following adequate laundering salvage prepackaged supplies in paper wraps that are not damaged, exposed to water or extreme moisture, or in a molded environment discard items if there is any question about integrity or mold exposure dry essential paper files and records (professional conservators may be contacted for assistance)

- Electrical medical equipment check motors, wiring, and insulation for damage inspect equipment for moisture damage clean and disinfect equipment following manufacturers' instructions do not connect wet electronic equipment to electricity

- Structures inspect, repair, or replace wallboard, ceiling tiles, and flooring repair, replace, and clean damaged structures

VI. Review Issues for Reopening Facilities

- Requirements needed prior to opening a facility potable water adequate sewage disposal adequate waste and medical waste management

- Have all areas to be opened been thoroughly dried out, repaired, and cleaned?

- Does the number of air exchanges in areas of the facility meet recommended standards?

- Are negative-pressure rooms functioning properly?

VII. Site-Specific CheckList for Selected Areas of the Facility (see attachment A)

Use the checklist to assist in determining if the facility is ready to be opened.

VIII. Post-Reoccupation Surveillance

Focused microbial sampling may be indicated to determine if:

- the water in the facility's water distribution system meets the microbial quality of the Safe Drinking Water Act (see: http://www.epa.gov/safewater/sdwa/index.html);

- mold remediation efforts were effective in reducing microbial contamination in the affected areas of the hospital (see: http://www.epa.gov/mold/mold_remediation.html);

- or if patients who are receiving care in the reopened facility acquire infections that are potentially health care associated and that may be attributed to *Aspergillus* spp. or other fungi, non-tubercular mycobacteria, *Legionella*, or other waterborne microorganisms above expected levels.

IX. Site-Specific Checklist for Selected Areas of the Facility

Attachment A

AREA	QUESTION	YES	NO	COMMENTS
Laboratory Services	Can essential laboratory testing be provided?			
	• blood-gases and co-oximetry • electrolytes • hepatic and basic metabolic profiles • hemograms and coagulation studies			
	Can microbiological, toxicological, and serologic testing be performed or sent to a referral laboratory?			
	Is emergency power available to operate equipment and safety systems and/or provide necessary ambient conditions?			
	Has essential equipment been inspected for damage and heat/humidity exposure and manufacturers contacted for guidance on repair, cleaning, and disinfection?			
	Have damaged or contaminated reagents and supplies been replaced?			
	Have biologic safety cabinets been cleaned, disinfected, and recertified?			

AREA	QUESTION	YES	NO	COMMENTS
Central sterile processing area	Have all autoclaves been inspected for sterile damage and manufacturers contacted for guidance on repair, cleaning, and disinfection?			
	Does the steam system meet AAMI standards? Have mechanical and biological indicator tests been performed on sterilization equipment?			
	Were stored sterile supplies compromised?			
	Have they been reprocessed or replaced?			
	Have the washers, instrument disinfection, and ultrasonic equipment been tested for performance?			
Operating Suite	Has there been any damage to the sealed flooring and ceilings?			
	Do sterile supplies need reprocessing?			
	Have the autoclaves been inspected and undergone mechanical and biological indicator testing?			
	Has an evaluation for electrical hazards been conducted?			
	Are the scrub sinks functioning properly?			
	Are there enough air exchanges per hour?			
	Have all air filters been changed?			
Pharmacy	Have damaged or contaminated medications and solutions been replaced?			
	Are refrigerators for medication storage at the proper temperature?			
	Has the medication compounding area been thoroughly disinfected?			
	Has the admixture hood been recertified and filters changed?			

AREA	QUESTION	YES	NO	COMMENTS
Respiratory Therapy, Bronchoscopy, Pulmonary Function Radiology, Radiation Oncology	Has the equipment processing equipment been inspected?			
	Was there any damage to equipment? Has it been repaired and certified?			
	Have damaged or contaminated medications and solutions been replaced?			
	Has all equipment been inspected and disinfected?			
	Have all damaged or contaminated medications and supplies been replaced?			
	Has damaged equipment been recertified?			
	Have radioactive materials been assessed and contained?			
All Patient Care Areas	Has all furniture and equipment been inspected, repaired, and disinfected?			
	Has porous furniture that was wet been discarded?			
	Were mattresses discarded if they have been under water or wet?			
	Have all linens been laundered?			
	Have medications and supplies that were damaged or contaminated been discarded?			
	Are medical gas and suction systems operable?			
	Have ice machines been flushed, cleaned, and disinfected?			
	Are medical gas and suction systems including air lines operable and cleaned?			
Emergency Department	Have stretchers and exam tables been inspected, repaired, and disinfected?			
	Have cardiac monitors been recertified?			
	Has the trauma room flooring been damaged?			
	Has it been repaired or replaced?			

AREA	QUESTION	YES	NO	COMMENTS
	Have support service areas in the ED (radiology, lab) been inspected in the same manner as the larger department?			
	Is public access to the emergency room safe for entry?			
Intensive Care Units/Burn Units	Have cardiac monitors been recertified?			
	Have whirlpool and physiotherapy area been repaired and disinfected?			
Laundry Processing Area	Has all laundry equipment been inspected for damage and manufacturers contacted for guidance on repair, cleaning, and disinfection?			
	Have containers for stored laundry chemicals and dispensing equipment been inspected?			
Food Service	Has stored food (dry and canned goods) been inspected for damage or contamination and discarded if it is unsafe to eat?			
	Have ice machines and refrigerators been cleaned and sanitized?			
	Has all perishable food been discarded?			
	Have all food contact surfaces been cleaned and sanitized?			
	Have pest control systems been restored?			
	Has local food service certification been obtained?			

Source: Centers for Disease Control and Prevention http://www.bt.cdc.gov/disasters/hurricanes/katrina/reopen_healthfacilities_checklist.asp

JCAHO Guidance on Emergency Planning

Key stakeholders in defining the community

- Public safety and security (fire, law enforcement, emergency medical services)
- Public works (roads, bridges, dams, transportation, sanitation, post office)
- Public health (immunizations, food safety, animal safety, epidemiology/disease surveillance, laboratory services)
- Schools, colleges, and universities
- Housing agencies
- Utilities (energy, water, communications)
- Health care providers (including, among others, hospitals, skilled nursing facilities, ambulatory and rural health clinics, rehabilitation centers, mental health facilities, and home care agencies)
- Private industry (for example, chamber of commerce, local industries, corporations)
- Service (for example, Scouts, Lions Club) and religious organizations (for example, churches, synagogues)
- Federally funded local response initiatives (for example, Metropolitan Medical Response System, Medical Reserve Corps, and Community Emergency Response Teams)

Participants at the planning table

Representatives from the following areas should be brought together as planning partners:

- Local government (mayor, village manager, or other elected official)
- Fire
- Law enforcement
- EMS
- Search/rescue agency
- Transportation
- Public health

Chapter 4: Plans and Procedures

- Public schools
- Housing agency
- Utilities (gas, water, electric, telecommunications)
- Local or regional FBI office
- Health care (ambulatory care, rural health
- clinic, hospital, long-term care, rehabilitative, mental health, home care, laboratories)
- Private industry (e.g., chamber of commerce, local industries, corporations)
- Special-needs populations (children, elderly, non-English-speaking, disabled)
- CERT
- Citizen Corps/Medical Reserve Corps
- Colleges and universities
- American Red Cross
- Media and communications (print, radio, TV)
- Mutual aid partners outside the community
- Civilians

County and state plans and planning initiatives

Examples:

- In Illinois, the West Central Municipal Conference has created a regional Homeland Security Coordinating Committee, which includes the mayors of 38 communities, some large and some small. Among other activities, this committee monitors allocations and expenditures by local, state, federal, and private entities for homeland security and develops and influences policies, protocols, and coordinated efforts.

- The Mayoral Institute for WMD (Weapons of Mass Destruction) and Terrorism Incident Preparedness, provided through the Idaho Institute of Emergency Management, provides the nation's mayors a "mayors only" forum to discuss strategic and executive-level issues and challenges and to share proven strategies and practices related to WMD/terrorism preparedness.

Chapter 4: Plans and Procedures

- The Peoria County Emergency Services and Disaster Agency, in Peoria, IL, coordinates all phases of comprehensive emergency management, defined by agency as mitigation, preparedness, response, and recovery, for Peoria County. It functions collaboratively within a five-county region to integrate planning response across multiple jurisdictions.

- Missouri's Department of Health and Senior Services has a close working relationship with the Missouri Hospital Association (MHA). Three MHA planners work with the 144 member hospitals and coordinate hospital planning efforts, assuring that hospital representatives are at the local, regional, and state planning table and linked to each plan.

Sample steps toward creating written emergency operations plan

- Develop a rough draft of the basic plan to serve as a point of departure for the planning team.

- Develop agendas and invitation lists for the cycle of planning meetings.

- Conduct a presentation meeting, establish committees for parts of the plan, appoint committee chairs, and schedule a follow-up meeting.

- Work with committees on successive drafts.

- Prepare necessary graphics (for example, organizational charts).

- Produce a final draft and circulate to the draft planning team for review and comment.

- Hold a meeting to incorporate final changes, discuss an implementation strategy and necessary distribution, and obtain informal commitments to provide information that could necessitate revision.

- Obtain concurrence from organizations identified responsibilities for implementing plan.

- Obtain official promulgation of the plan by elected officials and advise the media of this advance.

- Print and distribute the plan, with a copy (or release) to local media. Maintain a record organizations and persons that received a copy/copies of the plan.

Adapted from Federal Emergency Management Agency: State and Local Guide (SLG) 101: Guide Hazard Emergency Operations Planning. 1996. pp. 2-12. www.fema.gov/rrr/gaheop.shtm (accessed February 2005).

Hospital Preparedness Statistics

PERCENTAGE OF URBAN HOSPITALS THAT REPORTED SPECIFYING IN EMERGENCY RESPONSE PLAN TO CONTACT THE SPECIFIED ENTITIES DURING AN EMERGENCY, BY STATE

State	Law Enforcement	Fire	EMS	HAZMAT	Other Hospitals	Public health agencies	Other state and local government agencies	Other laboratories	Public private utilities
Alabama	94.5	89.0	89.0	89.0	89.0	81.9	94.5	48.8	63.3
Arizona	100.0	100.0	94.4	81.6	94.4	94.4	83.2	74.1	81.6
Arkansas	93.7	93.7	93.7	87.4	93.7	93.7	87.4	40.4	85.6
California	94.1	92.9	96.4	89.9	86.3	97.2	85.8	45.8	70.0
Colorado	93.5	94.0	68.1	94.0	87.9	100.0	94.0	45.8	80.4
Connecticut	100.0	100.0	100.0	100.0	100.0	94.4	77.8	70.6	83.3
Florida	95.9	97.3	94.7	95.9	91.4	93.9	97.0	58.8	73.0
Georgia	93.7	100.0	96.5	94.5	89.8	90.9	93.5	64.1	78.6
Illinois	92.5	88.1	92.6	84.6	94.1	94.1	78.8	58.5	66.2
Indiana	91.4	94.3	94.3	91.1	91.4	94.3	91.1	60.2	79.9
Iowa	90.0	90.0	90.0	90.0	90.0	80.0	80.0	80.0	100.0
Kansas	100.0	100.0	100.0	100.0	87.5	100.0	100.0	62.5	87.5
Kentucky	89.1	83.6	83.6	76.6	83.6	89.1	100.0	61.7	67.2
Maryland	100.0	95.2	100.0	90.5	81.0	100.0	95.2	57.1	85.0
Massachusetts	100.0	96.8	96.8	96.8	77.4	100.0	93.3	71.0	80.6
Michigan	92.1	100.0	88.9	89.5	92.1	97.4	92.3	62.2	81.6
Minnesota	100.0	100.0	100.0	94.1	94.1	94.1	76.5	41.2	56.3
Mississippi	91.0	91.0	100.0	70.5	100.0	100.0	100.0	67.6	70.5
Missouri	82.3	89.4	88.4	81.3	84.3	88.4	81.3	46.0	70.7
New Jersey	97.7	95.3	95.3	95.3	90.7	88.1	90.7	61.9	86.0
New York	100.0	100.0	95.1	91.8	86.1	98.5	95.6	58.9	70.1
North Carolina	95.8	95.8	91.7	83.3	87.5	87.0	91.7	47.6	82.6
Ohio	96.4	92.7	94.5	90.9	94.4	94.5	92.7	57.7	81.5
Oklahoma	92.2	92.2	92.2	92.2	100.0	100.0	92.2	81.6	92.2
Oregon	75.6	75.6	75.6	100.0	67.4	100.0	67.4	34.9	59.3
Pennsylvania	92.7	97.1	95.7	95.7	86.8	95.6	95.7	58.0	80.0
South Carolina	100.0	93.0	100.0	93.0	100.0	93.9	100.0	38.3	87.8
Tennessee	100.0	90.4	93.6	89.5	90.4	100.0	96.8	75.7	74.9
Texas	90.0	90.4	90.3	88.3	80.3	90.6	86.8	56.2	76.3
Utah	100.0	100.0	91.1	100.0	93.1	100.0	84.2	34.0	84.2
Virginia	96.1	92.1	100.0	88.2	100.0	95.9	92.1	64.9	81.3
Washington	91.0	91.0	86.5	86.5	95.3	100.0	85.9	53.3	53.3
West Virginia	100.0	100.0	100.0	100.0	100.0	86.3	100.0	63.7	54.9
Wisconsin	96.8	96.8	90.3	93.5	87.5	90.0	90.6	45.2	65.6

Source: United States General Accounting Office: Report to Congressional Committees. Hospital Preparedness: Most Hospitals Have Emergency Plans But Lack Certain Capacities for Bioterrorism Response. August 2003.

Department and Unit Disaster Sub-plan Templates

Patient care unit sub-plan template
Department/Disaster Call Tree

Department/Unit: _____   Department/Unit Manager: _____

Coordination Center: _____   Coordination Center Phone Number: _____

Chain of Command/Call Tree
(Include phone numbers)

```
              Manager/Dept. Head
             /                  \
      Asst. Manager          Charge Nurses
                            /            \
                     Support Staff   Administrative Staff
```

Call tree is updated at least annually.

DEPARTMENT DISASTER RESPONSE SUB-PLAN (BEDDED PATIENT CARE UNITS)

Department/Unit: _____   Department/Unit Manager: _____

Coordination Center: _____   Coordination Center Phone No.: _____

Situation requiring emergency response	Responsible person	Response
		RED ALERT
Fire Location: unit	Person discovering the fire. Responsibilities will be delegated by the Charge Nurse RN, CP, MR, SA RN, CP Charge Nurse RN, CP, MR MR, CP Charge Nurse Charge Nurse, MR MR	1. Rescue anyone in immediate danger 2. Activate nearest fire alarm pull station. 3. Contain the fire by closing doors, etc. 4. Extinguish if able to do so. Evacuate if there is immediate danger. 5. Shut off the medical gas zone valve location _____. Provide portable oxygen for patients requiring support. 6. Evacuate unit as instructed by Hospital Administration or Public Safety personnel. Evacuate immediately if there is immediate danger from fire or smoke.

Chapter 4: Plans and Procedures

Situation requiring emergency response	Responsible person	Response
		RED ALERT
Fire Location: unit	Person discovering the fire. Responsibilities will be delegated by the Charge Nurse RN, CP, MR, SA RN, CP Charge Nurse RN, CP, MR MR, CP Charge Nurse Charge Nurse, MR MR	**Evacuation Procedures** 1. Move Ambulatory patients, with medical records, to _____. An appropriate member of the staff will escort and remain in attendance. 2. Move Non-ambulatory patients, beginning with the least critical, to available rooms on _____. An appropriate member of the staff must remain with patients as determined by the patient's condition. 3. Coordinate vertical evacuation with the Emergency Operations Center. If building evacuation is required, the designated evacuation site is _____ 4. All medical records must accompany patients to their new location. 5. Patient transfers will be tracked in the Evacuation Log. 6. Perform a head count to ensure all patients/visitors/staff are accounted for. 7. Provide evacuation/patient tracking info to the Bed Control at 3-1510. 8. Ensure that service providers are aware of patient location – pharmacy, lab, physicians, respiratory therapy, and the Emergency Operations Center.
Fire Location: other unit/ department within same building	Charge Nurse RN, MR, CP, SA RN, MR, CP, SA RN, MR, CP, SA	1. Clear hallways 2. Close all doors on the unit 3. Prepare to receive patients from unit involved in the Red Alert 4. Limit phone use to emergencies only 5. Remain on the unit until the Red Alert has been cleared
		YELLOW ALERT
Mass Casualty	Charge Nurse	1. Determine bed availability Number of vacant beds Number of patients that can be immediately discharged Number of patients that can be triaged to another unit/ facility Ability to staff all available beds

Chapter 4: Plans and Procedures

Situation requiring emergency response	Responsible person	Response
		ORANGE ALERT
Mass Casualty	Charge Nurse - "notify management staff" Charge Nurse RN, Cp CP, SA MR RN, CP, AS Charge Nurse MR	1. Determine bed availability in collaboration with resident and report bed status to Bed Control. 2. The Incident Commander will determine the need to discharge or triage patients off the unit and will inform the Charge Nurse. 3. Consider the need to relocate visitors to the 2nd floor cafeteria. 4. Identify the amount/type of patient transportation equipment needed/available on the unit. Contact Patient Transport if additional transport personnel are needed. 5. Patients who are immediately discharged from the unit should be taken to the Discharge Coordination Center in the main lobby of the TVC. 6. Patients received on the unit during the mass casualty event will be admitted using the routine procedure. 7. Assess the need for additional supplies and notify the Service Center. 8. Reallocate all non-essential personnel to the Labor Pool, TVC 2703. 9. Activate unit call tree when advised by the Emergency Operations Center. Called-back staff should report to the Unit Coordination Center located at _____, phone number _____.
		YELLOW ALERT
Tornado	Charge Nurse RN, MR RN, MR, CP, SA RN, CP RN, MR, CP, SA	1. Inform patients of the threat of inclement weather. 2. Ensure that hallways are clear. 3. Assess the mobility of the patients on the unit and prepare for moving into safe areas. 4. Obtain extra blankets and pillows as needed for immobile patients.

Chapter 4: Plans and Procedures

Situation requiring emergency response	Responsible person	Response
		ORANCE ALERT

Tornado	Charge Nurse
	
	RN, MR, CP, SA
	
	Charge Nurse
		1. Move all patients and visitors into "tornado safe" positions.
		   Ambulatory patients should be moved into the hall away from windows and glass. Shut the door to the patient room.
		   Non-ambulatory patients should be turned away from the windows with curtains closed and head protected.
		   Visitors should be directed to the most interior area of the unit.
		2. Staff should remain in the interior areas of the unit as much as possible without compromising patient care.
		3. Remain in the "tornado safe" areas until the All Clear has been announced.
		4. Prepare to activate the Mass Casualty plan if necessary.

		YELLOW ALERT
Electrical failure	Charge Nurse MR RN, MR, CP, SA	1. Determine status of unit/department electrical system. 2. Notify Plant Services at 22041 of electrical system failures/problems. 3. Verify that all essential equipment is plugged into a red outlet.
		ORANGE ALERT
Electrical failure	Charge Nurse MR RN, MR, CP, SA RN Charge Nurse Charge Nurse Charge Nurse Charge Nurse	1. Determine status of unit/department electrical system 2. Notify Plant Services at 22041 of electrical system status. 3. Verify that all essential equipment is plugged into a red outlet. 4. Verify all equipment with battery backup is functioning properly. 5. Reallocate all non-essential personnel to the Labor Pool at 2703-4 TVC. 6. Establish contact with assigned Plant Services floor monitor. 7. Consider the need to relocate visitors to the 2nd floor Cafeteria. 8. Activate unit call tree when advised by the Emergency Operations Center. Staff should report to the Unit Coordination center located at _____.

Situation requiring emergency response	Responsible person	Response
		YELLOW ALERT
Oxygen failure Medical air failure Vacuum failure	Charge Nurse	1. Determine status of unit/department electrical system. 2. Notify Plant Services at 22041 of electrical system failures/problems. 3. Verify that all essential equipment is plugged into a red outlet.
		ORANCE ALERT
Oxygen failure Medical air failure Vacuum failure	Charge Nurse MR MR RN, CP CP, SA Charge Nurse Charge Nurse Charge Nurse Charge Nurse Charge Nurse, MR	1. Determine status of unit/department under alert. 2. Notify Plant Services at 22041 of any system failures/problems. 3. Notify Respiratory Therapy at 835-5978 (supervisor in charge). 4. Determine state of unit/department medical gas zone valve position. The zone valve is located at _____. 5. Obtain portable oxygen cylinders and regulators from the Service Center. 6. Consider the need to relocate patients to areas unaffected by the event. 7. Evacuate unit as instructed by Hospital Administrator or Emergency Operations Center. 8. Coordinate vertical movement of patients with the Emergency Operations Center. 9. Reallocate all non-essential personnel to the Labor Pool at 2703-4 TVC. 10. Activate unit call tree when advised by the Emergency Operations Center. Staff should report to the Unit Coordination Center.
		YELLOW ALERT
Water outage	Charge Nurse	1. Determine status of unit/department water system. 2. Notify Plant Services at 22041 of problems/service failure.

Chapter 4: Plans and Procedures

Situation requiring emergency response	Responsible person	Response
		ORANGE ALERT
Water outage	Charge Nurse MR RN, MR, CP, SA CP, SA CP, SA Charge Nurse Charge Nurse Charge Nurse Charge Nurse Charge Nurse, MR Charge Nurse, MR	1. Determine status of unit/department water system. 2. Notify Plant Services at 22041 of problems/service failure. 3. Advise all staff/patients/visitors to avoid hospital water supply/ice machines/ flushing toilets. 4. Verify that all water faucets are turned off. 5. Obtain water-less hand cleaner from Service Center. 6. Identify area for bottled water delivery. 7. Consider the need to relocate patients to areas unaffected by the event. 8. Coordinate vertical movement of patients with the Emergency Operations Center. 9. Reallocate all non-essential personnel to the Labor Pool at 2703-4 TVC. 10. Establish contact with assigned Plant Services floor monitor. 11. Activate unit call tree when advised by Emergency Operations Center. Returning staff should report to the Unit Coordination Center.
		YELLOW ALERT
Steam failure	Charge Nurse	1. Determine status of unit/department steam/heat system. 2. Notify Plant Services at 22041 of unit problems associated with steam system failure.
		ORANGE ALERT
Steam failure	Charge Nurse SA, CP Charge Nurse Charge Nurse	1. Determine status of unit/department steam/heat system. 2. Notify Plant Services at 22041 of unit problems associated with steam system failure. 3. Be conservative in the use of sterile supplies and linen. 4. Conserve heat in patient care areas. 5. Obtain blankets from unit stock and Linen Distribution. 6. Reserve the use of blankets for patients only. 7. Consider the need to relocate patients to areas unaffected by the event. 8. Coordinate vertical movement of patients with the Emergency Operations Center. 9. Reallocate all non-essential personnel to the Labor Pool at 2703-2704 TVC. 10. Establish contact with assigned Plant Services floor monitor. 11. Activate unit call tree when advised by the Emergency Operations Center. Recalled staff should report to the Unit Coordination Center.

Chapter 4: Plans and Procedures

Situation requiring emergency response	Responsible person	Response
		YELLOW ALERT
Steam failure	Charge Nurse	1. Determine the status of unit/department phone system. Check phones with different trunk lines "343," "322," and "936." Use alternate phones if only one trunk line is not operational. 2. Limit the use of phones to business only. 3. If all phones are down, confirm that the unit "red" phone is working.
		ORANGE ALERT
Steam failure	Charge Nurse Charge Nurse Charge Nurse MR	1. Determine the status of unit/department phone system. Check phones with different trunk lines "343," "322," and "936." Use alternate phones if only one trunk line is not operational. 2. Limit the use of phones to business only. 3. If all phones are down, confirm that the unit "red" phone is working. 4. The "red" phone, overhead public announcement system, and pager system are only to be used for URGENT patient care issues. 5. Designate a "runner" to deliver non-urgent communication between units/departments/etc. 6. Other "red" phone numbers are located in the Safety and Disaster Manual. If a "red" phone you are trying to reach is inoperable, try the regular phone number for that area. 7. Reallocate all non-essential personnel to the Labor Pool at 2743-2704 TVC. 8. Activate unit call tree when advised by Emergency Operations Center. Recalled staff should report to the Unit Coordination Center.
		YELLOW ALERT
Pager/ beeper outage		1. Restrict the use of paging system to emergency use only.

Disaster Preparedness for Healthcare Facilities

Situation requiring emergency response	Responsible person	Response
		ORANGE ALERT
Pager/ beeper outage	Charge Nurse MR Charge Nurse Charge Nurse, MR Charge Nurse	1. Confirm the availability of an appropriate number of staff/ physicians in the area. 2. Utilize other methods of contacting staff/physicians (office, home, cell phone). 3. If other methods are unsuccessful in contacting someone on the pager system, notify the hospital operator. Contact the Emergency Operations Center if the EOC is open for assistance with locating essential staff. 4. Inform staff that are assigned pagers that the system is inoperable and instruct them to check in regularly with the unit/department. 5. In collaboration with the Emergency Operations Center, determine the need to reallocate staff/physician resources.

Thompson's Healthcare Library

FREE 30-DAY REVIEW

❏ Guide to Medical Privacy & HIPAA
D'Arcy Guerin Gue and Steven J. Fox

Provides all the information you need to ensure that you're fully in compliance with the HIPAA privacy, security, transaction and provider identifier rules. The *Guide* also provides valuable guidance to help you prevent lawsuits and discusses your legal liability. Each chapter of the data-packed *Guide* provides thorough and up-to-date information.

D'Arcy Guerin Gue is Executive Vice President with Phoenix Health Systems, Inc., a firm expert in strategic planning, procurement, implementation and integration of state-of-the-art healthcare information technology. ***Steven J. Fox*** is a partner with Pepper Hamilton LLP and leads Pepper's health care informatics initiative.

Only $399 plus $24.50 shipping & handling.

❏ OSHA Guide for Health Care Facilities
Thomas H. Wilson

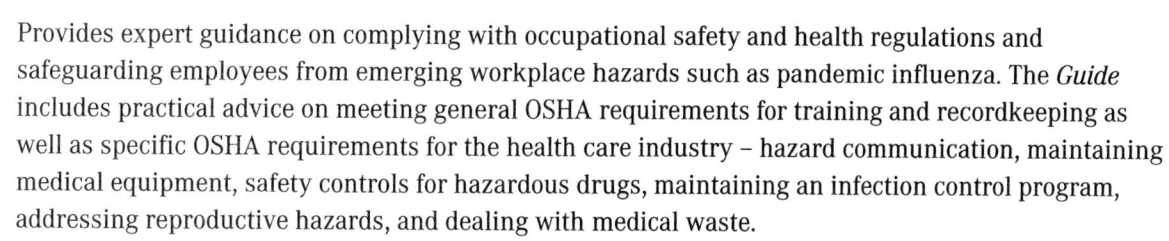

Provides expert guidance on complying with occupational safety and health regulations and safeguarding employees from emerging workplace hazards such as pandemic influenza. The *Guide* includes practical advice on meeting general OSHA requirements for training and recordkeeping as well as specific OSHA requirements for the health care industry – hazard communication, maintaining medical equipment, safety controls for hazardous drugs, maintaining an infection control program, addressing reproductive hazards, and dealing with medical waste.

Thomas H. Wilson is a partner with the nationally known law firm of Vinson & Elkins, L.L.P. He concentrates his practice in labor and employment law.

Only $499 plus $24.50 shipping & handling

❏ Nursing Home Regulations Manual
Robert J. Fogg

Provides comprehensive guidance on the federal long-term care survey, certification and enforcement regulations that nursing home providers must follow for Medicare and Medicaid participation. The *Manual* guides you through the evolving resident assessment instrument, including the latest minimum data set and quality indicator changes. It also assists you in preparing for surveys and appealing unwarranted deficiency findings.

Robert J. Fogg, of counsel to Archer and Greiner, P.C., in Princeton, N.J., is a recognized authority on health care law and regulations affecting long-term care facilities. Mr. Fogg formerly served as a state licensing director responsible for regulating nearly 1,100 health care facilities in New Jersey.

Only $379 plus $24.50 shipping & handling

Each annual subscription includes a looseleaf manual, regular updates and newsletter

To start your RISK-FREE trial subscription:

Call: 1-800-677-3789 • **Online:** www.thompson.com • **E-mail:** service@thompson.com

ⓘ THOMPSON